VASILI
THE LION OF CRETE

Murray Elliott

D1331753

CENTURY HUTCHINSON

Century Hutchinson New Zealand Ltd.
An imprint of the Century Hutchinson Group.
191 Archers Road, P.O. Box 40-086, Glenfield, Auckland 10.

Century Hutchinson Ltd.
62-65 Chandos Place, Covent Garden, London, WC2N 4NW.

Century Hutchinson Australia Pty. Ltd.
16-22 Church Street, Hawthorne, Melbourne, Victoria 3122.

Century Hutchinson South Africa Pty. Ltd.
P.O. Box 337, Bergvlei 2012, South Africa.

This edition first published in 1987
© Murray Elliot 1987

Second edition published in 1992
by EFSTATHIADIS GROUP S.A.

Third edition published in 1998
by EFSTATHIADIS GROUP S.A.

**Fourth edition published in 2000
by Efstathiadis Group S.A.**

© Efstathiadis Group S.A. 2002

© For the Greek market
by EFSTATHIADIS GROUP S.A.

ISBN 960 226 348 2

For Paul, Gregory, Martin and Rosalynd —
fortunate to have enjoyed an age without war —
and dedicated to Cretans and New Zealanders,
Australians and Britons whose courage, sacrifice
and honour vanquished a ruthless foe and welded
a bond of fellowship in adversity that has
endured three generations.

The youth who has never aspired to ride the clouds unfurled
Of what use is his life to him, of what use is the world!

— Cretan *distich* or *mantinade;* these rhyming couplets
epitomise the traditional heroic ideal of *levendia* — the gallant
attitude to life.

CONTENTS

FOREWORD

I had the honour to know Dudley Perkins — 'Kiwi' to his British comrades-in-arms — during the last six months of his life: all too short a time, but long enough to appreciate his exceptional qualities and to form a deep affection for him. In Crete, an island renowned for the valour of its inhabitants, the memory of 'Vasili' — Kiwi's local *nom-de-guerre* — is still revered.

Of his life before the war, I knew nothing; for he never spoke about himself. Actions to him were more important than words, and his courage was matched only by his modesty and reticence. But I often wondered what sort of background and upbringing had produced the man whose character and exploits were an inspiration to us all.

Murray Elliott's book provides the answer, but it is not for this alone that I welcome and recommend it. It also gives a vivid description of clandestine activity in enemy-occupied territory and, above all, it pays tribute - inevitably inadequate, for in Kiwi's case no praise could be enough — to a man whose manifest potentials were tragically cut short by an untimely, violent and heroic death.

Xan Fielding
Ronda, Spain

PREFACE

The world in which Dudley Perkins fought and died has been reconstructed from the memories and recollections of many people — Cretans, New Zealanders and Britons — and from documents, journals and published material (English and Greek), military reports, photographs and maps.

All the names, places and dates are real. Interviews were recorded and translated when necessary.

Some people, four decades later, possessed remarkable memories, describing incidents, physical features, dress, movements and speech in detail. But the memories of others have been tarnished by time. The author found that a few inaccurate versions of incidents have been perpetuated as they passed from mouth to mouth, sometimes emerging in print.

Considerable care has been taken to verify information about events of those times in which Dudley Perkins was involved. Doubtful accounts, embroideries and so-called facts found to be incorrect have been discarded in the interests of producing as authentic a story as it is possible to get so long afterwards.

Difficulties have arisen in identifying accounts which appear to have passed into legend about a resistance movement that stirred the blood and imagination of a strongly nationalistic people and which deviated — however slightly — to produce a more colourful tale extolling the prowess and fighting qualities of irregular soldiers determined to defend their homeland and their families.

No apology is therefore made for variations from already published acounts; in no way do the true facts detract from the honour of the hundreds of *andartes* who rose against a ruthless oppressor as their forefathers through the centuries did so many times before.

ACKNOWLEDGEMENTS

I am indebted to Antonis G. Mitsides for his patience and time in translating tape recordings of interviews with several Cretan wartime guerrillas; also to George Pediaditakis and Jean P. Crawford for accompanying me to these interviews in the White Mountains and putting questions about the wartime resistance and Dudley Perkins' part in it. These meetings elicited many unrecorded details of events of those times which have greatly enhanced the legend of Vasili.

Gratitude is especially extended to Major Xan Fielding, DSO, who spent considerable time reading and rereading the manuscript and contributing to factual accuracy.

I am grateful to Marika Begg for translations of written Greek documents and material.

The assistance and encouragement of the Perkins family, especially Dorothy, his sister, have been crucial in the production of the story of Vasili.

> *Hitler, don't boast that you stepped on Crete.*
> *You found her unarmed with her children absent,*
> *In foreign lands, high in Albania they were fighting.*
> *But otherwise, you'd have seen war, how the men fight,*
> *How the Cretans fight on the island of Crete.*

— folksong of the Cretan resistance

ONE

Mission to Selino

*Crete has become a legend, an epic poem,
island of heroes and Freedom's temple.*

— Cretan *rizitika*

Probably the most unrestful place in the world — cradle of civilisation, potpourri of luxury and poverty, beauty and squalor, forever
clamorous, bewitching, maddening; without tranquility, harbouring ancient treasures of human achievement ... Cairo.

The new day blushed scarlet among the minarets. Shadowy figures bustled, taxi horns blared, market carts rumbled and asses
trotted with their human burdens. The city was vibrantly astir. Its
hot dry breath wafted the aromas of musk, glowing coals and
dung, while desert sand blown on the wind mantled this sprawling
caravanserai.

It was 1 July 1943. In the fashionable suburb of Heliopolis, a car
drew up outside a villa in Sharia Asmoun. Out stepped Major Jack
Smith-Hughes, at twenty-three director of the Cretan Section of
the Special Operations Executive in the Middle East, and Lieutenant-Colonel Tom (T.J.) Dunbabin. They strode quickly inside the
big house used as accommodation for British secret agents and
Cretan resistance fighters.

Three men awaited their arrival.

'All set?' asked the Major.

Two of the group gave a ready affirmative. One was Sergeant
Dudley Churchill Perkins, seconded from the 2nd New Zealand

11

Division for special duties in Crete, eager to return to the island where, for more than a year, he had been stranded after the battle of May 1941.

Taken prisoner after the fighting ended, Perkins was lodged in the temporary enclosure set up by the Germans as a transit camp for captured Allied servicemen. With many others he escaped, and for weeks and then months lived in the White Mountains of Western Crete, joining several hundred others who had avoided capture altogether. Eventually, he escaped to Egypt in a Greek submarine. Back with the Division, fit and strong after illness and deprivations on the island, Perkins' mind wandered back to Crete. He had a great admiration for the people's struggle for freedom from an oppressor, although this was nothing new for Cretans whose history had been one long fight against invaders. He felt he owed them something for the risks they took in sheltering, succouring and helping him during those months on the run, their own lives at stake if they were caught. Now the chance had come.

Returning with Perkins was a young Cretan, George Psychoundakis, who had enjoyed four and a half months leave and training in Egypt and Palestine. Psychoundakis was itching to get back to Crete and resume his work for the resistance against the Germans.

The third was an S.O.E. officer, Captain Sandy (A.M.) Rendel, who was accompanying them as conducting officer, responsible for seeing them safely to Crete.

Smith-Hughes and Dunbabin gave the trio last-minute information and orders. After a few pleasantries, Smith-Hughes and the three travellers were in the car driving down the wide Heliopolis boulevards where luxurious homes and spacious gardens slid by. Perkins might have reflected that somewhere here, in times long ago, rested the Biblical city of On, and later the Egyptian cult centre of the ancient priests of Re.

As they headed south towards the Nile, Western influences gave way to the world of Islam in the district of Al-Zahir, mosques overshadowing houses in cramped streets. Further on, in Al-Sharabiy-yah, they drew up at Mahattat Misr, Cairo's main railway station. There, Smith-Hughes bade them farewell. For him it was just another stage in his strengthening of the resistance in Crete.

Kilometre after kilometre of green flatness unrolled before them, fields of cotton and tobacco, groves of palms, plantations of peas, tomatoes, mud-brick villages of the fellaheen. Men in long white gallabiyehs and veiled women in black robes bent with prim-itive tools over furrows in the rich brown mud. This was one of the most fertile places in the world, hiding the remains of dozens of ancient tribal sites older than the Pyramids. The sun flashed on ir-rigation canals as lateen sails glided across the horizon, the boats invisible on numerous canals patterning the landscape. Feluccas crossing the Nile dominated the scene.

Near Alexandria, at Kafr el Dauwar, the travellers joined a troop train. Soon the verdant delta fields and palm trees were replaced by the dry earth, sand and burnished stone of the door-step to the great Western Dester.

Approaching El Alamein the train ploughed off the rails and saboteurs were blamed. Hours of waiting passed with little relief from the searing air of the barren wastes. Evening was closing in before the track was repaired; a replacement engine enabled the train to move on.

Perkins and his companions viewed the debris of the weeks of fighting around El Alamein — great areas of scrap iron, burned-out trucks and cars, battered tanks and field guns, chunks of air-craft, some tail up with nose buried in earth pocked with craters blasted out by shells and bombs. In the deepening dusk it made a ghostly scene, underlying the hideous futility of enmity and of bat-tle.

The men blessed the comparative coolness of the night, dozing as the train trundled on westward at no great speed. At dawn they reached Sollum, the end of the line: a convoy of trucks took the troops on the rest of their journey into Libya. The devastation of war still stretched around them, and minefields had yet to be cleared after the battles that had passed that way only a matter of weeks before.

Tobruk was a shambles, with few building left standing, the harbour a graveyard of rusting hulks. Flurries of sand whipped up from the desert, added to the heat of the day, made the three hundred bouncing kilometres in the back of the military truck something of a trial. Towards evening, at a high point on the road, they looked down with feelings of relief on a small town and harbour — their destination, Derna — cupped in a craggy section of the Libyan coast.

Like Tobruk, Derna bore its battle scars — houses now rubble, streets churned, twisted relics of fighting equipment. Yet the inhabitants were achieving some semblance of normality. Enterprising Arabs, never slow to let an opportunity slip, were back in business. Bars were open in buildings left standing, supplied from Cairo for eager army customers, and shops seemed fully stocked.

The truck with Perkins' party jolted through the war-torn streets to the waterside. The men hauled their arms and equipment from the vehicle and went aboard the naval motor-launch in which they were to travel to Crete. Anyone examining the bags they brought aboard might have been surprised to find that they included items not normally handed out from quartermasters' stores. Both Perkins and Psychoundakis were still in uniform, but in their packs were Cretan country-style, clothes which they would wear from the moment they stepped ashore on the island. They also carried forged German identity papers, pills for drugging the enemy and suicide capsules. Perkins had his sewn into the lapel of his coat for easy access; all he need do was bite it.

Rendel was harbouring a heavy bag of gold sovereigns and a wad of official papers to be handed over to the British Army Commander in Western Crete, Captain Xan Fielding. There were also blank identity papers and fascimiles of rubber stamps used by officials in several Cretan villages. A further eighteen bags contained food, clothing, equipment, explosives and ammunition for Cretan resistance fighters. Rendel had even included tins of asparagus to add a touch of luxury to Fielding's diet.

When their packs and equipment were stowed, the young Cretan wanted a last fling before returning to the island so the trio went ashore to sample the wares of the local hostelries. As Perkins, Rendel and Psychoundakis returned aboard that evening to sleep and await the order to sail, they fully expected to be in Crete in the next day or two. It was to be a month before they made their landing.

Next day, under a scorching noonday sun, the ship's captain took his small craft out of its haven into a gentle swell. The freshening wind brought up the sea and soon the launch was undergoing a severe buffeting. When progress became difficult, and it was evident the craft had no chance of reaching Crete in time for a night landing, the captain turned the boat round and headed back to port. Storms at sea continued for two days. Not until the weather improved could Headquarters in Cairo let Xan Fielding and his reception party in Crete know when next to expect Rendel and his charges.

Of great concern during this period of waiting was security — preventing enemy spies from perceiving that a mission to Crete was under way.

Eager though they were to be off, the party enjoyed their brief spell of freedom. They spent the time swimming and fishing, and eating in an army canteen. One day they visited the ancient Greek city of Cyrene. Rendel arranged for an army truck to take the three of them to the site some distance to the west of Derna. Wandering among the extensive ruins, he explained to them the archaeological significance of their various features.

When the weather abated, the order came from Cairo for them

to make another attempt. Meanwhile the craft in which they were quartered had developed a fault. With their gear transferred aboard another motor-launch, Perkins and his companions moved out early in the afternoon into a flat calm. The signs looked good and the passage proceeded smoothly; in the deepening dusk the White Mountains of Western Crete were just visible.

Because of the rumble of their craft's engines the approach of an enemy aircraft was not detected until it was almost above them. The roving German plane circled the launch for a few minutes before flying back to its island base. The pilot had made no attempt to dive lower for a closer inspection, but there seemed little doubt that the presence of the craft and the direction of its course would be reported. It was therefore deemed unwise to make the landing attempt that night, and in darkness they turned round and chugged back to base.

Fearing that the cloak of secrecy had been penetrated, and that enemy agents might have the craft under observation, the skipper was ordered next day to leave Derna and head east towards Alexandria. In a secluded bay, away from prying eyes, the anchor was dropped and there they waited while Cairo arranged another night for the landing. Southward, empty desert shimmered without sign of civilisation.

The order came a day later and the craft headed north again, this time in swelling seas. By mid-afternoon the launch was being tossed unmercifully and even the strongest stomachs were heaving. It was decided to turn back yet again and after an unpleasant battering the three passengers were glad to see Derna once more.

With the moon getting beyond its first quarter it became necessary to wait until it was well on the wane and the operation was temporarily abandoned. They left the ship with their equipment and piled into an army truck, driving out of Derna to an aerodrome where a Royal Air Force Squadron was based. There they were taken to a hut where they stayed alone, apart from the other

16

personnel, although they took their meals in the officers' mess. When Cairo was ready to move them again they returned to Derna and precautions were taken to ensure that their embarkation, in darkness, went unobserved.

It was a different craft from either of those used in the recent abortive attempts. Psychoundakis bubbled with excitement — it was the same one which had taken him from Crete to Egypt more than five months previously, and he greeted her with the kind of affection one reserves for old and trusted friends. The travellers were told by the skipper, Lieutenant Bob Young of Canada, that they must stay below. They had to remain out of sight, cramped and sweating, all night and until well after midday. The engines fired and the motor-launch was under way. It was 29 July — just four weeks and a day since they had set out from Cairo.

The initial course lay eastward, to mislead anyone watching with special interest; once out of sight of land the craft slewed north. Soon they discerned a large convoy of British ships bearing down on them and the skipper felt it best not to weave among them. He hove to in fine weather and calm seas until the convoy had passed by. The voyage continued with a blazing sun moving across deep blue sky. It was a glorious afternoon.

No patrolling German aircraft appeared to signal their approach; there was no need to man the anti-aircraft weapons and machine-guns with which the craft was liberally armed. In the fading light the 'Big Island' — as it is known to the Greeks — revealed its craggy crown, a distant hazy blur above the darkening sea. As Perkins gazed ahead into the twilight, he may well have recalled the words written by the Greek classical poet, Homer, in the *Odyssey*, Book XIX:

Out in the dark blue sea there lies a land called Crete,
A rich and lovely land washed by the waves on every side,
Densely peopled and boasting ninety cities . . .

17

The first indication that they were getting near land was when a long arm of light reached far out to them, passed slowly over the sea and dimly stroked the little ship. The German searchlight crew, operating either from shore or shipboard in the Gulf of Mesaras, apparently failed to sight the boat at so great a distance. Had the craft been heading for any of the landing places formerly used in the middle area it might well have been detected, but it was making for the more isolated south-west shore.

The shadowy island of Gavdos slid by to starboard, its small German garrison oblivious of the nocturnal passage of the enemy. According to the Acts of the Apostles, St Paul was carried here by a 'tempestuous wind called Euroclydon'. On this night Euroclydon – the violent north-easter known these days as the Gregale – was dormant.

Near the Cretan coast the captain slipped the engine into neutral while watchers on deck strained their eyes for torch signals. Then he made a slow sweep well out to the west, turned and cruised back. Nothing. Another traverse had just begun when a small ball of light stabbed the darkness, spelling out the agreed code.

Immediately the skipper headed cautiously towards the flashes, the screws turning slowly to keep their noise as low as possible. Massive rock cliffs loomed ahead – shadowy, mysterious, harbouring unknown dangers. But all was peaceful, the loudest sound the tranquil wash of surf on shore.

Had the party not turned back on the night it was spotted by German air reconnaissance the voyage might have ended very differently. On that occasion the reception party flashed the agreed signal on hearing the engines of a motor boat, uncertain that it was the British craft. Suspicion was confirmed when machine-guns spat and German voices called on the group to give themselves up. British agent Xan Fielding and his Cretan helpers were hardly able to scramble up the rocky cleft behind the landing site and es-

18

cape. By day, a seaplane was observed on patrol, dipping low near the beach and ravine of the location, an excellent place called Tripiti, almost inaccessible except for a narrow slit in the cliffs which could be scaled only at this one point by those who knew where to find it. Mountain patrols would not discover it, and the nearest German guard post was about three kilometres away at the tiny beach hamlet of Souyia. Now, the German watch on it from the sea made it unsafe and it had to be abandoned.

After careful scouting, a new place was chosen a few hundred metres to the west. Although closer to the guard post, this was a cave entered over deep water from the sea and undetectable from the land. Inside, it led to an opening high up on the mountainside. The gap was just big enough for a man to squeeze through and with brushwood as camouflage, the entrance was effectively hidden. The place was known as Kaloyeros (the monk).

Xan Fielding recalls that on the first night they expected the landing there, they had forgotten to bring a torch. The ingenious Cretans built a fire with brushwood and Sergeant Alec Tarves — his cover name was Little Aleko, but he was called Kalaidzis (the tinker) by many Cretans — masked the flame with his jacket, lifting it in jerks to simulate the morse signal. By the time they gave up, when no boat appeared, the occupants of the cave had nearly suffocated in the restricted space. Disappointed that their makeshift efforts had not brought a landing, they relished the knowledge that no German sea patrols now seemed to be operating.

Several days later, after a wireless signal from Cairo, the reception party moved down again from their mountain lair to the cave. This time they remembered the need for a signal light and brought two torches. For two hours they signalled intermittently before they were rewarded by the murmur of marine engines at slow spped.

When the Canadian skipper had got as close in as he dared, a dinghy was lowered and two sailors rowed Perkins, Rendel and

Psychoundakis ashore to a wild welcome from exuberant Cretans.

'Kalispera . . . yassou, yassou.' Their joyful excitement was understandable after the weeks of waiting and the scares the German had given them.

The homecoming for Psychoundakis was emotional, intoxicating. He broke into song, a favourite English ditty among several he had been taught by British comrades.

> *Hitler has got only one ball*
> *Goering's got two, but very small*
> *Himmler's got something similar*
> *But Dr Goebbels got no balls at all!*

First to land was Sandy Rendel, met warmly by Fielding, surrounded by what looked like a band of brigands — about a dozen men in black shirts, black breeches with baggy knees, black tasselled headcloth and knee-high leather boots. Some had purple sashes wound round their waists, holding the typical long Cretan knife; others had ammunition bandoliers and carried firearms. They were the epitome of the traditional *pallikaria* — medieval foot soldiers — still a term in general use to denote brave and manly fellows.

Psychoundakis bounded ashore to be embraced with vigorous bear-hugs by everyone — Fielding, Alec Tarves the wireless operator, George Phindrilakis from George's own village of Asi Gonia, George Paterakis and his brother Andonis from the village of Koustoyérako, and several other Cretans. Among them were men Perkins already knew; for him, too, it was a kind of homecoming.

In the firelight Fielding first met the man who had been sent to be his second-in-command. Garbed in breeches and tattered jacket, looking much like the mountain shepherds amongst whom he would be moving, Perkins was observed as 'slim' and 'long-headed' by his leader, who said he was impressed by his quiet voice as he introduced himself, although he uttered only three words: 'I'm Perkins, Sir.'

Rendel, recording his own impression of that moment, saw Perkins as 'reliable and imperturbable amid the excitement, still reminding one, in his breeches and old jacket, of the open-air life of camping days near his native Christchurch'.

Rendel handed over the bag of gold and the messages from Headquarters and received a packet of reports and letters to take back. One gold sovereign in those days was worth several thousand drachma — enough to keep a family for many weeks.

Meanwhile, a well-tried method of ferrying the stores ashore from the launch was arranged, whereby a rope allowed the sailors bringing them in to haul themselves easily between ship and the cave-ledge. This operation took the best part of an hour. Bob Young called for Rendel to return to the motor-launch, anxious to be away. Fielding then remembered to ask for water to fill the group's flasks as no springs were nearby. But Young felt he could not risk staying longer and immediately started the engines. Soon their throbbing receded into the darkness.

The first task for the reception party was to get the stores to a safe place in case the Germans, who no doubt heard the launch from their post along the coast, should send out search patrols as soon as it was daylight. The heavy packages were hauled up to the narrow exit from the cave onto the mountainside and then buried among the rocks. Meanwhile some of the men set off to get donkeys to help haul the stores and equipment to the campsite.

For the whole of that first day the newcomers remained hidden in the cave. At dusk men returned with donkeys and the packages were retrieved and lashed to the animals' wooden saddles. The donkey team then began its trek through the darkness, taking the precious cargo over a roundabout route which would be easier for the beasts and safer for the men.

Perkins and his companions slept that night in the safety of the cave. They crawled out at dawn and prepared to leave for the camp above Koustoyérako. As they began the climb to the hide-out, Perkins had a feeling of being 'back home', among friends he had come to admire and love. Fourteen months earlier he had been a straggler after the German occupation of the island and had despaired of getting away. Now things were different. He had a purpose, a mission, an assignment — a job to do with despatch, a contribution to make to the war in a manner which suited his temperament. And he could give practical aid to those who had fed and sheltered him while he was on the run.

TWO
Eager and Determined

Mother, the country calls me, as a soldier they will dress me. I leave you, my sweet mother, come and bless me.

— Cretan *mantinade*

Dudley Churchill Perkins was in the forefront of those who volunteered for service with the New Zealand Armed Forces after the outbreak of the Second World War. He joined up on the first day for enlistments in Christchurch, 16 September 1939, his regimental number being 1772.

Up to that point fighting a war was probably farthest from his thoughts. The second son of an Anglican parson, Dudley was born at Tapanui, Otago, and attended Balclutha District High School. Later he went to Hokitika District High School, moving with the family to his father's next parish.

At the age of fourteen Dudley lost his father, who died of cancer. It was the period of the Depression and the family fell on hard times. His mother, Adelaide, brought them all to Christchurch. After a spell at Christchurch Cathedral Grammar, Dudley received financial assistance to attend Christ's College for three years.

He is remembered as being quiet, clever, studious and determined, and in 1932 passed the matriculation examinations. Although he wanted to go to university, circumstances dictated that he should work to contribute to the family's living. At that time the eldest brother, John, was studying for the ministry to follow in his father's footsteps.

Tavronitis
Chane
Maleme•
Galatas•
Kisamos
Bay
Falasarna•
Kastelli
•Platanos
Alikianos•
Mesara
Bay
Lakkoi—Meskla•
Karanos•
Zourva•
Stephanoporo—Tromarissa•
Prases•
kefali•
•Elos
•Stroves
Gingilos•
Omalos•
•Stomiou
Kandanos
Achlada•
•Vothiana
Pytharaki•
Moni
•Moustakos
•Mploma
•Chrisoskalitisis •Homishana
Nerospili•
•Psilafi
Sklavopould
Rodavani•
Moni •
•Voutas
Lividas• •koustoyerako
•Prodromi
Pikilasos
Elefonisi
•Koundora
Souyia•
Aghia
Roumelli•
Tripiti
Paeochora
Kaloyeros

Crete

Akrotiri
Peninsula

Souda   Souda Bay

• Kambos   • Neo Chorio
kona • Kyriakoselia
  • Tsakistra   Nippos
                    • Vrises
            • Vapes

Rethymnon

                • Episcopi
          • Kournos
              • Argyroupolis

ite Mountains

            • Asi Gonia
  • Askyfou   • Alones
        • Kalikrati
              • Tsilivdika
      • Manika
                            • Selia
Chora Sfakia   • Rodakino   • Plakias
                                    Preveli
                                    Monastery
                        Limni

Dudley joined the Christchurch firm of Pyne Gould Guinness, stock and station agents, where he worked as a clerk for six years. Then, when John had completed his studies, it was his turn for higher learning. He began an Arts course at Canterbury University where a degree may well have been the first step in pursuing a career with the church. One of his subjects was Ancient Greek, the starting point of an interest in the language as spoken today. But he was there for only two terms when war broke out and he left to enlist.

It may be wondered why a man whose father preached peace on earth was motivated to join up to fight a war on the other side of the world with what may seem undue haste and little consideration. This was something his mother and family asked him too. In his quiet manner, without histrionics, he told them: he left he had a duty to do.

He was sent north for his initial training, begun on 3 October at Hopu Hopu Military Camp, near Ngaruawahia. He was home for Christmas on final leave and sailed with the First Echelon on 5 January 1940. Cairo, which he came to know well, was reached on 12 February — eleven days before his twenty-fifth birthday. There he was taken on the strength of the 4th Field Regiment and served in both E Troop and the headquarters unit of 26 Battery. The equipment was 25-pounder artillery.

For some thirteen months his unit underwent fairly solid training, with manoeuvres in the desert in preparation for the action to come. There were brief spells of leave in Cairo; extended leave was largely a matter of luck. It was customary for the names of two men to be drawn from a hat each week for seven days' leave at Sidi Bishr rest camp in Alexandria. In June, out came Perkins' name and that of Bombardier Rod Matheson. With leave passes and rail warrants they took the train to Alexandria on Saturday 5 June, anticipating pleasant relief from camp discipline.

The next day, Sunday, they felt there might be some advantage in attending church. Matheson said he had heard that servicemen standing around outside afterwards were often invited home by local people. They did this and were approached by a very well-dressed European lady who invited them to lunch — if they had no other engagements! A sleek limousine materialised and wafted them off to the home of the British Consul, to which they were invited to return for dinner the following Thursday. They had evidently made a good impression!

On that night, halfway through the meal, the Consul was informed that Italy had declared war on Britain, and all service personnel were to return to their units immediately. He told Perkins and Matheson not to bother — he would telephone the camp to fix it so that they need not return until midnight. The two men stayed to finish their meal and to enjoy a leisurely evening and were driven back later in the Consul's limousine.

Nine months were to pass before there were signs that Dudley Perkins was at long last to get a crack at the enemy. He sailed in March with Lustre Force to Greece and soon found himself close to that country's northern borders with Albania, Yugoslavia and Bulgaria. His first taste of action came in April, 1941, when the great tide of German might rolled over the borders and began sweeping the Allied armies before it. Perkins is recorded as having shown his mettle in action at Pinios Gorge on 17 and 18 April, his troop sergeant-major, Vic Rowland, stating that 'among many very gallant young gentlemen his thoroughness, determination and reliability were outstanding. He discharged his duties under fire with the coolest sangfroid and aplomb.'

From Pinios Gorge, near Mount Olympus, Perkins' unit was among those which withdrew south and took up defensive positions at Molos, some 160 kilometres north-west of Athens. Hitler's panzer divisions drove relentlessly on, supported by continual bombing and strafing from a superior Luftwaffe. For two hours on the evening of 24 April Perkins and his comrades fired against targets while they still had ammunition. Then they removed the breech blocks and abandoned their guns, using their trucks to withdraw towards their allotted evacuation beach.

On the night of the 25th, according to Lieutenant Ian Johnston, they rested in the hills near Athens. The 4th Field Regiment had become somewhat fragmented.

Battered Commonwealth and Greek forces were evacuated in a variety of craft — naval and merchant vessels of Britain and Greece, and caiques, the small Greek fishing or sailing vessels. German bombers sank several of these vessels but many got through to Crete or to Egypt. Most of Perkins' troop reached the beach at Porto Rafina, south-east of Athens, on 26 April and were taken off by the destroyer *Khandahar,* sailing into Souda Bay, in Western Crete, the next day. Other men in the regiment boarded vessels which landed them in Alexandria.

With units forced to leave behind their guns and many of their rifles, their trucks, equipment and food stores — in the interests of saving the men — the troops who arrived in Crete were illprepared to fight again. Among the last to arrive was the Division's Commander, General Bernard Freyberg. He regarded the disembarkation of the Division in Crete as a mere stepping-stone to getting his men back to Egypt, to re-equip and retrain and to prepare for participation in the defence of the Middle East. But he had been less than two days on the island when the Middle East Commander, General Wavell, arrived and informed him that he was appointing him to the command of all the forces then in Crete, and that he was to organise that island's defence.

Freyberg told Wavell of his desire to move the New Zealand Division back to North Africa without committing them to battle in their present state, deficient in arms, artillery, equipment and transport. Wavell replied that he thought Crete would be attacked in a matter of days and it was Freyberg's duty to stay and handle the task. Explaining his acquiescence later, 'Tiny' — as this big man was affectionately known to his men — said he could do nothing but accept.

It is no part of this account to recreate the battle for Crete, or detail the events in which Perkins was merely one of nearly 42,000 defenders. Several works totalling many hundreds of thousands of words have been written about that epic struggle and questions posed as to why the Allies lost, and where lay the blame. General Freyberg's own official report on the battle and his preparations for it is still a secret document, unlikely to be released before 1993. In the meantime, it seems clear and fair to say that blame for the defeat in Crete cannot be placed at the door of any one man or group of men. Blunders were made from the very top, by governing politicians, right down to commanders in the field. Most of these can be excused, labouring as the leaders did under all kinds of handicaps. Only the soldiers and their officers closest to them can be said to be entirely blameless — they did what they could without the means to do it, and they nearly succeeded.

If Freyberg, the New Zealand Government, and military leaders in the Middle East had had their way, Crete would have been left for the Germans to overrun. Only a day after taking command in Crete, Freyberg telegraphed Wavell, now back in Egypt, to the effect that 'forces at my disposal are totally inadequate to meet attack envisaged'. But the decision to stay and fight was a political one: Churchill was determined that a stand should be made in Crete, to demonstrate British determination to the Americans, and to show loyalty and support for the cause of the Greeks.

In early May, 1941, there were some 30,000 New Zealand, Australian and British servicemen on the island. Of 11.000 Greek soldiers, 3,700 were garrison troops, the rest being escapes from the mainland. Some of the British troops had been on Crete for six months, ostensibly to prepare a defence, but inept leadership and lack of proper directives meant that little had been accomplished.

Such large numbers should have been more than sufficient to

overwhelm the 7,000 invaders of the German 7th Airlanding Division. But the enemy had the sophisticated weaponry of a modern, efficiently trained and well equipped force. The Greek garrison had only one First World War weapon for every six of its men; the 7,000 who escaped from the mainland came mostly without arms of any kind. Later, when rifles became available for distribution among the Greeks, they were of five different types with only enough ammunition for a few rounds to each man. Nor were the British and Commonwealth troops much better equipped. Artillerymen had to leave their guns behind on mainland Greece, trucks and other vehicles and heavy equipment had to be abandoned. Many of the survivors from Greece arrived with only the uniforms they wore, although some had disobeyed orders to throw away their arms and came with a rife, a Bren gun or a mortar. Also lost were the field kitchens, and the medical and hospital services were largely without their supplies and equipment. After the debacle of Greece, morale was low and the survivors believed Crete to be a transit point for movement to North Africa. It came as a shock that they were to defend the island against imminent attack.

The New Zealand Division was given the sector between Chanea, then the island's capital, and the airfield at Maleme, a coastal stretch of about 20 kilometres. Hard on the heels of the disorderly arrival and in the ensuing confusion Freyberg planned a defence he hoped would repel the German invaders and deny them victory. He had one big stroke of luck — Wavell had presented him with documents giving him almost exact plans for the German attack. Detailed were the number of aircraft and gliders to be used, the type of troops to be employed and their numbers, the targets of the attack and the bases from which it would be mounted. In addition, Freyberg knew the timetable for the invasion; as the forces were being assembled he was kept informed of changing times and dates as the Germans made final preparations.

This coup was made possible by the work of military intelligence units based in Bletchley in Buckinghamshire, where British experts, only a few weeks before, had been able to crack the German military codes by a system known as Ultra. Now, another monitoring station at Abbassia, near Cairo, using the same system, was listening in to German military traffic in the Balkans and North Africa and decoding it in quick time to give field commanders up-to-date information on German intentions. Freyberg now knew that the attack was to be made jointly by paratroops and by an assault from the sea. Stressing the inadequacy of his forces, he pointed out the necessity for both air and naval support if any defence was to be successful.

Two days later Wavell promised naval forces to deal with the sea invasion and indicted somewhat enigmatically that while air defece could be crucial, he thought the reported scale of the Germans' airborne attack was exaggerated. He doubted that troops could be removed from Crete before the Germans mounted their assault, and he added that his instructions from the War Cabinet were that Crete was to be held. Shortly afterwards Freyberg received a personal message from Churchill which attempted to allay the commander's fears. Churchill also told the New Zealand Prime Minister, Peter Fraser, that the enemy would have no tanks or artillery and that the close combat of the type envisage should suit the New Zealanders' fighting capabilities!

Freyberg then set about deploying his forces. As the defenders made their preparations they were under constant air bombardment and were continually strafed. Ships bringing much-needed arms, ammunition and equipment to Souda were sunk both in port and at sea. To counter these air attacks Freyberg had only six Hurricane fighters and seventeen obsolete Fulmars and Gladiators. No reinforcements came from squadrons in North Africa and by 18 May — two days before the German invasion — only four Hurricanes and three Gladiators remained to repel the might of the Luftwaffe.

Although few digging tools were available, slit trenches were prepared. The small number of Bofors anti-aircraft guns of British and Australian units were placed around Malene airfield. Aircraft-smen without machines to service were drafted as infantrymen and given rifles. British ships which succeeded in berthing at Souda brought in more rifles and ammunition, but some men were still without weapons. Right through the whole regimen of military paraphernalia there were vital deficiencies. Trucks to deliver supplies were few and dive-bombers destroyed some of them. Equipment for communications was quite inadequate: there were not enough radios, wireless sets and field telephones to maintain efficient contact and in the event some of these proved faulty.

Perkins found himself among troops near the village of Galatas, five kilometres south-west of Chanea, as a member of what was quaintly known as the 'infantillery'. These were men without guns and equipment who were reorganised into what was officially labelled the Composite Battalion. They were mainly artillerymen, but some sections were made up of men from the Army Service Corps.

Perkins' group of 'infantillerymen' was stationed a little more than a kilometre north-west of Galatas, close by a feature militarily labelled Red Hill. Sergeant-Major Vic Rowland recalls: 'Perkins was one of ninety-eight men with me. Our weapons were just fourteen rifles, some pistols, a few machetes and some clubs cut from olive trees. We had no bayonets.'

There is little doubt that Freyberg made the best use of the limited resources at his disposal. Had he the aircraft to combat the Luftwaffe, the battle could have been over almost before it started. Even so, with all the limitations in arms and equipment, his strategy should have been well-nigh perfect to beat back those paratroopers who made a safe landing. Forces were dispersed to protect the airfields at Maleme, Rethymnon and Heraklion, the town of Chanea and the port of Souda from airborne attack; units were also placed strategically to deal with invasion from the sea, expected on the beaches between Chanea and Maleme. Plans included a method of dealing with the initial onslaught which was to be directed mainly at Maleme, arrangements for counter-attack should parachutists land in undefended territory west of the airfield and beyond defended localities, and protection as far as possible for Souda.

Early on the morning of Thursday 20 May, Dornier bombers, Messerschmitt 109 fighters and Stukas bombed and strafed Allied positions as they had done many times before. Most of the troops took it to be the usual breakfast-time harassment. Soon the attackers broke away and silence settled through the dusty air. A low drone became audible. As it grew louder the clear blue sky to the north became a speckled black, resembling a flight of birds. These were Junkers 52 transports, some towing gliders. It was just 8 a.m. General Freyberg was having breakfast with a British officer, Captain Montague Woodhouse. Freyberg is said to have looked up and remarked: 'They're dead on time.'

Half an hour earlier Perkins and his 4th Field comrades had ended their early morning stand-to. When the alarm went only pickets were left on Red Hill. They manned their positions and fired shots at aircraft and at a few paratroopers who landed near them, but for most of the day they had little action, and moved about a lot on patrol. Some who failed to have a tilt at the enemy felt emotionally cheated.

An idea of what the defenders faced can be gauged by the scale of the first waves of aircraft sent over on that beautiful warm and sunny morning. General Kurt Student, at his headquarters in Athens, committed nearly 1,200 aircraft to this initial assault: 280 bombers, 150 dive-bombers, 180 fighters, 500 transports and about 75 gliders. As the transports discharged their human cargoes the heavens over north-western Crete, from the Akrotiri Peninsula to the Tavronitis River, became filled with dark forms dan-

33

gling under parachutes, green, brown, white and black. Many of the descending enemy were picked off — one man likened it to the opening of the duck season in New Zealand. Other Germans died as they struggled out of their harness on landing. As well as the gliders, some transports crash-landed, their occupants sprayed with Bren gun fire before they could emerge. Enemy dead were soon lying all around.

A number of paratroops, however, landed away from their intended dropping zones and were able to regroup without harassment for organised attack. New Zealand units deployed to repel the sea assault when it came, but held in reserve to deal with paratroops landing in undefended areas, were not immediately brought into play. The reason was apparently partly due to misunderstandings after a breakdown in communications when runners and signal flags had to be used. Had the enemy been prevented on landing from regrouping beyond the defences, it seems likely that the Allies could have won the day.

A combination of factors then lost the defenders the battle. To begin with, lack of air support gave the Germans complete mastery of the skies. On the ground the Allies were handicapped by shortages or arms, artillery and ammunition, an almost complete lack of tanks and armoured vehicles, few trucks and malfunctions in the small numbers of radios and wireless sets. There also seems little doubt that misunderstandings and delays due to inadequate communications contributed to one of the chief causes for the loss of the battle — abandonment on the second day of Kavkazia Hill (labelled by the defence strategists as Hill 107), the key position for the defence of Maleme airfield.

Stationed on the hill and commanding an unobstructed view of the aerodrome was A Company of 22 Battalion, along with the battalion commander, Lieutenant-Colonel Les Andrew. When his positions came under attack from infiltrating Germans, his men suffered heavy casualties and he called for reinforcements. These failed to arrive and, judging his situation to be untenable, he pulled out. The Germans advancing up the northern slopes were astonished to find empty trenches. The position which controlled Maleme airfield was in their hands, less than twenty-four hours after the initial onslaught.

German historians agree that had the New Zealanders counter-attacked around the airfield and on Kavkazia Hill, the paratroopers would have been overwhelmed. After their heavy casualties of the previous day their numbers were few and they had all but exhausted their ammunition. While many blame Andrew for the loss of the hill, Freyberg does not. Years later he wrote that he himself took full responsibility for the policy of holding the airfield. Colonel Andrew 'was given an impossible task ans he has my sympathy'.

Two other factors contributed to the failure to hold the island. One was leaving the airfields intact after the RAF had no further use for them, possessing no serviceable aircraft. Mining or obstructing them would have denied the Germans an immediate ability to land troop transports. The other was the failure to commit the reserves soon enough to their secondary role of reinforcement and conterattack. This allowed Student to reinforce his beleaguered troops with ease, and from then on the German build-up was unrelenting.

These reserves, dug in to meet a searbone invasion, were never needed for that purpose. On the night of 21 May heavy gunfire was heard out at sea and a red glow pierced by rockets and flares spread across the sky to the north. The Royal Navy had intercepted the enemy flotilla — some twenty-five ships and small boats shepherded by an Italian light destroyer, carrying the heavy artillery of the German Mountain Division and 2,300 men. The German convoy was no match for the British Navy. About two-thirds of the invasion force were sunk or left burning; none reached Crete.

Freyberg — who had expected a much larger invasion fleet with about 10,000 men — was greatly relieved the next day to learn that the threat from the sea had been removed. He could now concentrate on counterattacking the paratroop force, moving forward from a defensive role. But with the Germans reinforced and able to land aircraft on the aerodrome, the best efforts of the Allies were too late.

For two-and-a-half days it appears that Perkins and his companions had little to do except watch and wait. Patrols sent out encountered only light resistance. Some troops found that if they placed a black swastika on a white background German planes would drop them food, wireless sets and arms.

On the afternoon of 22 May Perkins' unit had to take cover from the Luftwaffe which appeared in force and bombed and strafed their area. On·23 May things became livelier with enemy infiltration. (The Germans believed they were up against a highly skilled force in cleverly entrenced positions, manned by first-class infantrymen with picked marksmen, since so many of their casualties had been shot through the head). By 24 May German paratroops around Galatas had been reinforced by crack alpine soldiery. The Luftwaffe was very active, bombing and strafing the New Zealanders' positions. In the afternoon the enemy were testing the defences with limited success. Meanwhile, Perkins' section mainly men of the 4th Field, moved to north of the town.

Next day the Germans made a concerted attack on Galatas. This followed intense bombing and aerial machine-gunning. Vic Rowland recalls that his unit was ordered to make that would have been a bayonet charge — if they had had any bayonets! Even so, with some losses, his men managed to check the German advance in his sector, although only for a short time.

The battle raged back and forth, around and through Galatas during the afternoon and night of 25 May — remembered as one of the great actions of New Zealand war history. Late in the afternoon the Germans drove the New Zealanders out of the village.

The New Zealanders were hastily regrouped by the 10th Brigade Commander, Brigadier Howard K. Kippenberger. With bayonets fixed, they charged back into Galatas, chorusing blood-curdling Maori was cries. Spearheading the attack were two British tanks commanded by Lieutenant Roy Farran. In a fierce battle fought mostly hand-to-hand, with heavy casualties on both sides, the New Zealanders retook Galatas — only to be told a few hours later to withdraw because of a lack of reinforcement. Men have been moved to poetry and historians to eloquence in describing that bayonet charge. Out of it emerged a reputation for the New Zealand Division as a 'terrible killing machine.'

By the morning of 26 May the story of the Composite Battalion was ended. Small groups became intermingled with others in a retreat which now became inevitable. Chanea was ablaze. Ships burned in Souda harbour, some for several days. Roads were pocked with bomb craters and raked continually with machine-gun fire by an unopposed German air force. The Allied armies were in disarray, bombed and strafed as they fled south over the White Mountains to the evacuation beach at Sphakia. This, in spite of the Germans having understimated the garrison strength in Crete, and not expecting such stiff resistance.

At the same time the forces at Heraklion, numbering about 4,000, abandoned their airfield and left in British naval ships. And at Rethymnon the Australians surrendered the airfield to superior forces.

From Sphakia nearly 12,000 men were embarked over four nights. Nearly 1,800 of those evacuated were wounded. Over 6,000 were left on the shore, among them a disappointed Gunner Perkins. He was among the many who were captured on 1 June after the departure of the last evacuation ship. Some evaded capture then and took to the hills.

During the battle and after the evacuation more than 12,000 Allied servicemen were taken prisoner. The Allied dead numbered

1,751; at sea, the Navy lost about 2,000 seamen.

The Battle for Crete, though a defeat in itself, was not wholly unproductive for the Allies. Freyberg's men gave Student's paratroopers such a severe mauling that Hitler abandoned plans to use them in an attempt to capture Malta in the same way, and the British island was spared invasion.

The Germans have borne down with a thousand aeroplanes.
They throw down cannons, soldiers with parachutes
To take Crete and to enslave her.
Fly away, bird, to your plain and tell your people
To endure the war until we come down,
And show the corsair Germans how Crete makes war,
How the fights and how she strikes for her freedom.

— Cretan *rizitika*

THREE
On the Run

To be abroad, to be an orphan, to be sad, to be in love,
Put them in the scales, and the heaviest is to be abroad.

— part of a Cretan song of *xeniteia* (exile)

Perkins was among several thousand Allied servicemen marched back over the mountains from Sphakia after failing to be taken aboard the evacuation ships. Unshaven for a fortnight, exhausted and unwashed, they joined prisoners taken during the battle in Dulag Kreta — a makeshift prison camp on the coast at Galatas, four kilometres west of Chanea. This had been hastily prepared on the sites of the 7th General Hospital and a children's holiday camp, Paidiki Exokhi. Intended as a transit camp (the prisoners were to be moved to holding areas on mainland Greece and to permanent camps in Germany), the only shelter provided was a few bivouac tents, and when the newcomers from Sphakia arrived conditions became chaotic.

Most men had to sleep in the open with no cover by day from the searing sun. Hunger gnawed at their guts after an absence of food on the march and little in the camp. Water came from a single well of the type once worked by an ox; for this there were interminable queues.

Many dead from the battle still lay unburied and the sickly stench of rotting flesh pervaded the camp area. Buzzing blue-bottles, flies and mosquitoes added to the men's discomfort. Several hundred reported sick every day; some lay down and died —

exhausted by lack of food, the arduous trek over the mountains to Sphakia, and the trudge back again as captives. Morale was at a low ebb, but being on a beach prisoners were able to bathe, keep clean, and stay free of vermin.

Over the next ten days officers and NCOs attempted to establish some sort of order. Tents were salvaged to put everyone under canvas. Burial parties were organised; groups were sent out to forage for food and to recover rice and other supplies from Allied dumps. After the removal of Australians to another area, some five thousand men remained, nearly a third of them New Zealanders. Meanwhile, the Germans had flown out seriously wounded men to the mainland.

No prisoner avoided disease. Every man had at least one bout of dysentery and scabies. Several suffered from malaria and there were a few cases of poliomyelitis.

German rations distributed were totally inadequate for a sustaining diet. Survival was assited by sympathetic Cretans who were permitted to deposit baskets of food at the camp fence. But still this was not enough. Individually, and in small groups, prisoners crawled nightly under the wire, evading lax guards as they dived into vineyards and olive groves in search of food. They experienced no difficulty in returning with their spoils, guards giving them a wink if they were noticed.

This situation changed some weeks later when the German paratroops and alpine battalions were sent to the Russian front and irresponsible young soldiers took over garrison duties. They wounded and killed a number of New Zealanders by indiscriminate schooting. Cretans were forbidden to bring food to the prison camp fence and some who carried on regardless were also shot. When complaints were made to the German general in command he blamed Crete's climate as affecting the soldiers' nerves!

Before then, however, the appaling conditions invited escape. Wire strung around the camp would scarcely have kept cattle from

40

wandering, and many men who broke away did so merely because they could no longer stand the poor rations.

In the early days, too, no proper registration of prisoners was made; nor were names passed on to the Red Cross. (For some such notification did not happen for up to six months, when they reached a permanent camp.) Officially, Perkins was posted as 'missing'.

Dudley Perkins was among the earliest of escapees. He had been in the camp about a fortnight when he and Tom Moir, a staff sergeant in the 5th Field Regiment, were in a group of a dozen prisoners who broke camp on 18 June, crawling in darkness under the wire and disappearing into the olive groves. There the escapers split into groups of twos and threes, as it would be easier for small numbers to get food and shelter.

Perkins and Moir headed west with fellow artillery man Jim Hughes who was limping badly. Suffering from a leg wound, Huges found it difficult to keep up although his companions were carrying his haver sack. Rather than delay their progress Huges returned to camp and escaped again when he was fitter. In a village near Maleme airfield Perkins and Moir found their first benefactor who provided them with food. They ate avidly, but unaccustomed to the oily Greek preparations, suffered afterwards. For two or three days they stayed in hiding and then with the help of a guide, they made their way to the rugged and scantily populated west coast.

There they felt luck was with them. They discovered a boat — not the best for the journey to North Africa, but good enough for an effort as desperate as theirs — and they made their preparations. From friendly Cretans they collected food and water, a blanket or two to use as sails, and other useful items. After a few days they were almost ready to leave when a message came to them that a German patrol had found the boat and had impounded it. It was the first of many disappointments.

41

Soon their hopes were buoyed again when word came of a party, which was making ready to leave from the south coast from a beach near Souyia, some eighty kilometres away. Carrying much of the food and the gear they had collected, they set off south through the mountain chain and reached the beach after several forced marches.

Disappointment again awaited. They found the party wet, exhausted and depressed. An Army Service Corps man, John Kerr, told Perkins and Moir how they had bought a boat for a small sum of money. When they put to sea they discovered its flaws and before they had gone very far a plank gave way and the craft became waterlogged. After struggling for some hours they managed to manoeuvre the boat back to the shore. Before they reached land, a German patrol boat passed by further out to sea but presumably took them to be fishermen and did not investigate.

The boat was examined to see whether it could be repaired adequately for crossing the Libyan Sea, but they decided it was a hopeless task.

As Perkins and Moir were now finding out, escape from the prison camp was merely the first of several hurdles. Food and shelter were daily requirements. While the weather was fine they slept outdoors when darkness fell. It was high summer and warmer than they had been accustomed to in New Zealand, so sleeping rough was no hardship. Out in the open it was also easier to avoid German patrols.

Food was a different problem. Perkins was loath to put the lives of Cretans in jeopardy by constantly seeking food from them and attempted to live as best he could off the land. When he could not get food from the Cretans, he was reduced to living on snails and dandelion roots. Later, circumstances forced him to rely more on Cretan help.

Some evaders found Cretans unwilling to aid soldiers, believing they could be the enemy in disguise. Such suspicion and wariness

42

led some evaders to return north for a time to the area around Maleme where food was more easily obtainable. Clad in Cretan clothes they could move quite freely, although the Germans were all around them. Perkins and Moir on occasion risked eating in tavernas frequented by German soldiers.

Perkins moved higher into the mountains and, when he became ill through lack of proper food, was taken in by villagers. Like many another escaper he was nursed back to health and strength with meals of fresh meat, vegetables, eggs, fruit, goats' milk and cheese. The New Zealander discovered he was only one of several hundreds of evaders being cared for by the mountain villagers. Some were living in homes, others in caves of which Crete has more than 3,000. The Cretans — many poor and themselves facing hardships — became unstinting in their aid: as well as food, they supplied clothing and money. Many men who had suffered disease and malnutrition became fit enough to concentrate again on their main purpose — escape.

Soon after the evacuation from Sphakia, the Middle East branch of the War Office Intelligence Section began making plans to help escaped prisoners and stragglers who had evaded capture. In high summer, on 17 July 1941, Lieutenant-Commander Francis Pool landed from the submarine Thrasher at the Bay of Limni. Three Australians, flashing signals seaward in the hope of attracting a rescue craft, had been surprised to see the submarine surface; they gave Pool an appreciative welcome.

The Australians led Pool to the Lower Monastery of Preveli (now derelict) where Abbot Agathangelos Lagouvardos was conducting High Mass. The heavily-bearded abbot, black-cloaked, his impressive seal of office on a gold chain around his neck, suspected Pool of being a spy for the Germans. Although Pool had represented Imperial Airways in Eastern Crete for several years his appearance was not English. He looked more like a Cretan and he spoke perfect Greek.

Shortly, Abbot Agathangelos was convinced of Pool's identity and they began an association which was to have repercussions, some of which were bountiful, some tragic. Pool was put in touch with patriotic Cretans and soon small parties were being guided from their hiding places by the Cretan resistance, taken through the mountains from village to village and on to Preveli. The monastery and surrounding villages and countryside became a transit camp. The Abbot and his seventy monks housed and fed large numbers of soldiers.

The evacuation plans excited the many Allied troops roaming the mountains. When the news reached prisoner-of-war camps around Chanea, the inmates found the incentive to breach the wire or get away from labour gangs working outside. Ahead of them would be a trek of some 150 kilometres, the going very rough.

On 26 July messages that stragglers should be ready to leave went out to the villages of Ardaktos, Vatos and Fratti, where many Australians, escapers from the Rethymnon sector, were being cared for by Cretan families. As the sun vanished and the day's seering heat subsided the men emerged from hiding and made their way to the monastery. In starlit darkness the men, along with Cretan friends, made their way down to the beach.

An hour before midnight the submarine Thrasher appeared in response to flashed signals and stood off 100 yards away in a choppy sea. It was too rough to ferry the men in the submarine's small collapsible craft and a line was rigged to the shore to guide the men who were required to swim.

There were emotional scenes as the men, monstly Australians, prepared to leave. They embraced their newly-made Cretan friends, some of them comrades in battle, who had risked all to feed and shelter them. They shouted: "Thank you, thank you", and vowed to return one day.

Three New Zealanders and sixty-two Australians and British

clambered aboard Thrasher before its commander decided it was time to leave. They reached Alexandria on 31 July. Those left behind awaited their turn another time.

On the night of 18 August the submarine Torbay surfaced off Preveli to arrange another evacuation. Aboard were Lieutenant-Commander Pool and Sergeant George Bremmer of the Gordon Highlanders who was a member of the Special Boat Section. He had a folbot, a wooden-framed canoe like an Eskimo kayak which was propelled with a long double-bladed paddle.

Sergeant Bremmer was launched in his craft in rough water and was swept out to sea. Torbay got under way and rescued Bremmer. The sumbarine then moved closer to shore for Bremner to make a second attempt to reach the beach. He succeeded after an exhausting effort.

Meanwhile Commander Pool was landed with stores, including a wireless transmitter, for delivery to resistance groups.

Bremner brought an Australian and a New Zealander back to Torbay. They confirmed that many Commonwealth troops were awaiting rescue. Bremner also met Cretans ashore and asked them to alert stragglers that Torbay would return on the next night to take them aboard. When Bremner returned Torbay withdrew to submerge by day and wait.

On the next night Torbay returned and Lieutenant-Commander Tony Miers grounded the submarine's bows. Bremner took his folbot to the beach and brought back Pool who had completed his meetings with resistance fighters. Pool said that twenty-eight Commonwealth soldiers were ready on the beach. As the sea was rough and it would be too exhausting for Bremner to ferry them out, a floating coir rope was towed ashore by Bremner, assisted by naval engineer Tony Kidd, to guide the waiting men who were expected to swim. Bremner ferried in his canoe two or three who were wounded.

Miers was told that about a hundred more men could be taken

off if he could return for a third night. Torbay pulled away well before dawn to lie submerged for another day, safe from scouting German eyes and reconnaissance planes.

When Torbay returned on the night of 20 August many more than 100 men were waiting, not all of them Commonwealth servicemen. The rope was rigged between submarine and shore with inflated "Mae West" lifebelts assisting flotation. Bremner made thirty journeys with wounded and sick while fit men used the floating line. Several Greek soldiers came aboard, but as Commonwealth men had priority some had to be sent back to the beach. Apart from Pool and his party, Torbay lifted thirteen officers and 117 other ranks of whom 62 were New Zealanders. The 130 included eight Greeks and a Yugoslav. Embarkation that night was accomplished in less than two and a-half hours. Half an hour before midnight Torbay backed away. Monks from Preveli Monastery drove goats up and down the beach to obliterate evidence of the evacuation. Well away from Crete by dawn Torbay dived and landed her human cargo safely in Alexandria next day, 22 August.

For these and other operations Bremner received the Military Medal while Pool was awarded the Distinguished Service Order.

Before any more evacuations could be arranged, information spread by the word-of-mouth Cretan telegraph found its way to 'bad Cretans' — the local term for traitors — and eventually the German occupiers learned of the part played by the monastery at Preveli. One morning the monks awoke to find their sanctuary surrounded by German troops. None of the stragglers waiting to leave fell into the trap because precautions had been taken for them to remain hidden in the countryside, but the monastery was ransacked and property and valuables were confiscated. The Germans took away herds of goats and sheep and the monks' large store of food. The buildings themselves were wrecked and desecrated.

Abbot Agathangelos was able to escape, and British agents got him away to Africa. The monks, under interrogation, could therefore blame him with a clear conscience. Some were killed and others imprisoned at Chanea. At the tiny harbour of Limni, used for the evacuations, the Germans set up a guard post and that part of the coast became useless for evacuations.

By the end of August several hundred prisoners had escaped from Galatas. They moved south to join stragglers already roaming the foothills, the mountains and the upland plain of Omalos where shepherds tended their sheep, grew crops and made cheese.

With the arrival of garrison forces to replace the invasion troops, an intensive campaign was mounted to round up stragglers and escaped prisoners. During August and September many were caught on the south coast while awaiting a chance to get away from the island in small boats. At the end of October and late in November, thirty New Zealanders were in two parties taken off after a British naval officer was landed to organise the rescues.

Posters proclaimed death for anyone found harbouring stragglers or escaped prisoners. Leaflets were dropped by air exhorting men to give themselves up. They read:

Soldiers of the Royal British Army, Navy, Air Force!
There are many of you still hiding in the mountains, valleys, villages.
You have to present yourself at once to the German troops.
Every opposition will be completery useless!
Every attempt to flee will be in vain!
The comming *sic* winter will force you to leave the mountains.
Only soldiers who present themselves at once will be sure of a honourable and soldierly captivity of war. On the contrary who is met in civil clothes will be treated as a spy.

The Commander of Kreta

The large number of stragglers on the run led the Cretans to arrange a system of ensuring maximum help with minimum risk to themselves. They would decide how many men would be looked after by each village and, mindful of the activities and whereabouts of German patrols and search parties, they would move stragglers from one village to another. In those days only mule tracks linked the remotest villages.

As the resistance began to be organised with the guidance of British agents, stragglers were provided with forged identity cards, good enough to bluff the ordinary German soldier, but detectable in the hands of a security expert.

In this way Perkins moved across the White Mountains for several weeks. He came to know well what to expect in Cretan village homes. These mountain people led a much more frugal and tougher existence than any pre-war New Zealand farmer. Their houses were often no more than one or two rooms enclosed by whitewashed stone walls; many had stone floors — but in some of the poorer dwellings there was merely tramped earth and the roof might also be of earth held up by wooden poles laced with brushwood. Such houses contained little furniture, perhaps a table and two or three wooden chairs. Several people would sleep in one room on flimsy mattresses on the floor, or there might be halfway up a wall a curtained alcove into which a makeshift mattres was fitted.

A conspicuous item was often a chest in which was stored the marriage dowry, sometimes little more than some thick home-made woollen blankets. Cooking methods were primitive, employing a stove fuelled with wood and charcoal, the smoke escaping through an aperture in the roof. Villages still used *pitharia* (large earthenware jars) to store food. On the walls might be strings of onions and any other crops which could be stored in this way. Most houses would have a picture of the Virgin on the wall, perhaps with an oil wick beneath it. Faded pictures of fathers, grandfathers, brothers, unlces and cousins who were *pallikaria*, brave fighters of past times, would also find pride of place. In normal circumstances guns and other weapons would hang on the walls — not there for display, but because it was the handiest place to keep them.

Around the houses chickens pecked in the dirt; they provided eggs as well as an eventual meal. Goats were kept for milk, and a pig in an improvised sty would one day become a feast. The family might own two or three crop fields in widely separated areas — the resulf of more than one family inheritance. Inevitably, because of the system under which each man upon marriage is given a plot of his own, holdings become smaller. Though a man could gain more land through inheritance, the new acquisition might cause difficulties in husbanding it.

Sheep provided most of the available meat. Many upland villagers possessed flocks, kept near the village in winter, but taken to selected high areas in summer where sheepfolds and cheese-huts were permanently established and grazing available. Here, they sheared for the wool, spun by the womenfolk for clothes, and made cheese of the sheep's milk. During the occupation the Germans confiscated most of these flocks for their own larders, and at the end of the war scarcely and sheep were left. The ubiquitous donkey was an essential tool of the mountain villager — it provided transport over rough tracks in regions of no roads. And it carried the heavy loads — cheeses, fodder, and wood for fuel.

Though the villages often had little food after the Germans took what they wanted, and seldom had any to spare, they always found something for stragglers, even if they had to go hungry themselves. Perkins became accustomed to offerings of olives, cheese, *Khorta* (a spinach grass soaked in oil), occasionally an egg and honey, oranges, potatoes and rough country wine and *raki* (a warming homemade vodka-like spirit). Sometimes there was bread, but more often he was given *paximathia*, the hard rusk-bread baked twice — as it still is today, sold cheap in any Cretan bakery.

In a report he made after the war, Moir told of the occasion when villagers came upon him and Perkins unexpectedly while they were sleeping off the effects of a midday carousal. They were discovered in an olive grove and it was insisted that they stay. Cretans feel hurt if you decline their freely offered hospitality: for three days Perkins and Moir were plied with more food and wine than they wanted or was good for them, although it made up for the many lean times they had endured. But enough was enough. After the third night of eating and drinking they waited until the village had settled down to sleep then slunk away in the darkness. For several days afterwards they avoided areas of habitation until their food ran out.

Even in those early days of the occupation, the Cretans felt they wanted to do more to rid their island of the invader. Perkins was sometimes asked whether he would join them in a private war against the Germans. When they sought his advice he always cautioned them against any rash action which might prove fruitless and expensive in casualties. Ever mindful of the risks they took in sheltering and feeding stragglers, he never stayed long in one place. In this way he acquited a wide circle of Cretan friends willing to help him whenever he appeared.

Grateful for their help, Perkins admired the spirit of the Cretans and their long tradition of hospitality to strangers. In turn, the Cretans developed for this man a profound respect. In stature, Perkins was bigger and taller than most Cretan men and his ramrod bearing and strong, handsome facial features — resembling the portayal of many a Greek god — earned him instant esteem. For Perkins, it was a situation which made him feel humble, and he grew to regard the Cretans as he would brothers and sisters. They endeared themselves to him, and he to them. Stragglers who found that they were viewed with suspicion by Cretan upland villagers had only to mention that they knew Perkins to be immediately accepted as men in genuine need.

With so many of them moving around the mountains, Perkins and Moir realised that it was only a matter of time before the Germans would attempt to round them up. Their best chance of escape, they realised, still lay in being on the coast, and the odds would be improved if they were in an area where the Germans were thin on the ground. The ideal place was therefore Selino, the extreme south-western of Crete, remote, desolate, rugged, with sparse population.

The mountains there rise sheer from the Libyan Sea; inland, ravines slice through craggy rock walls. There is little good land for cultivation and there were few roads. Only mountain trails, trodden by goats and shepherds, linked many villages. Even today, man, beast and nature conspire to preserve a wilderness that spurns the seduction of modern progress, and one's foot occasionally strikes pieces of ancient masonry from a civilisation long since dead, relics of cities which enjoyed an honoured place in history.

The ruins of Tarrha, existing for a thousand years until A.D. 500, lie in the sands of a small beach. Several other cities — Elyros, Lissis, Hyrtakina, Syia and Poikilassos — formed with Tarrha the Confederation of Oreioi around 300 B.C., allied with the ancient Roman province of Crete and Cyrenaica, under King Magnus, whose capital was Gortyna, close to the middle of the island's south coast. The Lefka Ori men of Selino joined their neighbours in wars as well as trade.

Vardis Paterakis recalls meeting Perkins in the hills in the autumn of 1941 and telling him to go to the village of Koustoyérako and to seek out only his family — to go to no-one else. Perkins did indeed spend happy times there. Vardis says he was intrigued with the olive trees, which he had not known in New Zealand. Often he would sit under them with six or seven others eating dry rusks and olives.

Moving further to the west, Perkins and Moir stayed first in a picturesque, sheltered cove called Ktista, near Koundoura. It was at the extreme end of the south coast, its only building a hillside chapel. The nearest Germans, so far as they knew, were sixteen kilometres to the east, at Paleochora, which was occupied by army and navy personnel.

Jim McDevitt, of 20 Battalion, recalls his meeting at Ktista with the Dudley Perkins and their anguish in seeking a craft to take them to Egypt.

'He was a likeable sort of guy', says McDevitt, 'intelligent and of a bright disposition.

'Our living conditions were harsh — there were no villages or people nearby, no shellfish, no way to catch fish. We had only dandelions, carob beans and whatever else we could find — but I never once heard Dudley complain.'

Later, at Elafonisi, — an offshore island reached by wading through shallow water — they gorged on oranges washed ashore from German ships sunk by the Allies. Drums of fuel which also floated in helped to provide warmth in the winter months. Sometimes they could catch octopuses, and they found that tins dropped down with stones inside enticed young octopuses to settle there.

McDevitt adds that Perkins was indefatigable in his search for a boat, suffering 'many heartbreaking disappointments'. The only boats they saw at that time on the south coast were Italian and German patrol boats.

'Once we saw a cargo ship passing near the shore, but we had no way of reaching it. Again we had to watch helplessly one evening when a large illuminated vessel, with prominent Red Cross markings, passed tauntingly by.'

Later, Perkins, McDevitt and others made their way inland. In the course of time some of them made friends with families in the tiny village of Sklavopoula, about eighteen kilometres north of

Ktista. McDevitt says they often gathered at the home of Iphigenia (usually known as Fifi) Papantonakis, who did much to help the stragglers survive.

During the two years the men were roaming the Cretan mountains and coasts there were many daring escapes from the island. Some rowed; others used blankets for sails. Caiques with motors were stolen, while others joined Cretans and Greeks escaping in craft of various sorts. Altogehter, after the evacuation, several hundred managed to leave the island by such makeshift methods. Among them were some 200 escaped prisoners. These were the lucky ones; their comrades were often not so lucky and ended up in prison camps.

FOUR

Captain George — Opportunist

Give food to the hungry, to the tired give a sheet,
To the drinker food and wine for him to drink and eat.

— Cretan *mantinade*

Although Selino was the poorest part of Crete, people deprived themselves in order to ensure that their visitors were well cared for — such is Cretan hospitality. Life was hard at the best of times, but now under German oppression the burden of poverty became more acute as the occupying troops took crops and livestock.

Normal trade links with Greece were cut; in any case, Greece itself was depleted and had no food to spare for its islands. In addition, Crete had exhausted its own reserves during the winter to supply the Cretan forces then fighting in Albania. At times, all some Cretans had to eat were messes of seed potatoes and orange-peel tea, even though irrigation enabled them to grow three potato crops a year.

Escapers often needed to range far and wide in their search for food, and fortunate indeed were those who had a good pair of boots. Footwear soon became cut to pieces on the shale and rock of steep mountain slopes. During these days of roaming, often under mental as well as physical strain, the idyllic scenery of coast and mountain so reminiscent of life back home helped to relieve the pressures and allowed hope to persist.

Chances for picking up a boat continued to recur. Most of the craft along the coast had been systematically destroyed by the Germans, either by patrols on foot or by aerial gunfire. Others near villages and coastal garrison posts were kept under guard. Many attempts were made to seize them, occasionally with success. Some fishermen were permitted to keep their boats provided they took a German guard when they went out and handed over a goodly portion of their catch. There was always the chance that one of these fisherfolk could be persuaded to desert to Egypt and take some evaders with him.

It would be too much to pretend that none of these men — hundreds of them, British, Australians and New Zealanders — did nothing of which they might feel later ashamed. There were at times misunderstandings, and incidents arising from the actions of desperate men. One New Zealander who submerged himself in the village life has suggested that there were some who were plain lazy and caused trouble, while others saw themselves in the role of lone wolves, seizing or demanding instead of making approaches. Another who spent an equally long time at large is just as firm in his assertion that he knew of no such incidents, suggesting that if they did occur, they were not common. On the other hand, there were Cretans who refused help — some after they had seen the punitive actions of the Germans, and others who feared for their own future needs. It is easy to understand the attitudes on both sides and the final verdict must be made with reference to the high regard that New Zealanders and Cretans have for each other, to the post-war aid sent to the island, and to the number of Cretans who have made their homes in New Zealand.

Although there were hardships and many dangers, the monotony of the life was perhaps the worst to endure. There was often loneliness, which makes hardship more difficult to bear. For families back home the period represented a long blank of uncertainty. Months, or a year or two later, they might hear how so-and-so had been seen, or heard of, how a cave had been shared, a night spent at a campfire with shepherds and a flask of wine, how an attempt had been made to seize a boat, or of a fruitless wait for a rescue craft which never came.

On several occasions Perkins teamed up with Kerr; they shared a firm friendship and a common resourcefulness. Men like them were more successful in winning the confidence of the Cretans; in the contacts they made from village to village they learned how to live on the land and although this was sometimes difficult, both had experienced camping life in New Zealand. Lying on a rocky hillside in the sun, looking out to sea, it was easy to indulge in a moment's fantasy that they were in fact in the country of their birth. As they wandered the hills there were many scenes which could be briefly identified with home, but the resemblance was never complete. On the coast there was an unfamiliar scarcity of seabirds, and often there were periods of calm not experienced on New Zealand shores. Inland, there was an abundance of bird life, especially in autumn when vast flights would head southwards on migratory journeys to the Fayoum of Egypt, to the Sudan and further afield. Some of these birds were familiar from books — the nightingales calling in March, the swallows nesting in August. And though the sea might be still, the nights were not silent. From May to November there was always the sound of the crickets, particularly in the olive groves.

The search for food occupied much of their time. Sometimes eels could be caught, and large freshwater crabs which came out at night to forage near the banks of streams. Once or twice they joined a fisherman in the hazardous sport of dismantling mines around the coast, using the explosives to blast a haul of octopus, squid or other fish. They learned, too, how to make a meal with the aid of the fungus which grew near the roots of the olive trees. Boiled with tomatoes and onions, with olive oil added, it was quite delicious. There were also mushrooms to be found.

Less appreciated for the most part were snails. These were first boiled to remove the slime and then, after rinsing, were dropped still in their shells into a vegetable stew into which a liberal amount of olive oil had been poured. Meat was never plentiful, but occasional rabbits or hares could be snared. In Western Crete partridges and pheasants were fairly abundant, but this was sometimes a disadvantage as their presence attracted unwelcome parties of German hunters.

Mulberries, raisins or grapes were often to be had, and a kind of tea made from sage, or some of the German ersatz coffee made out of ground roasted acorns and barley. Of course there was wine, and the potent spirit tsikouthia, or ṛaki and ouzo. Such spirits were not always drunk. They might be rubbed into tender feet, or used as a skin lotion after shaving off a ten-day growth with a blunt German blade. They were also valuable for the rheumatics and lumbago which followed long exposure to rain and damp sleeping places.

It might seem that the men lived well, but such items did not figure on the menu every day and they were hungry more often than not. Like squirrels, they stored chestnuts, eating them roasted, or grinding them into a flour with which to bake. Almost every evader experienced a period of near starvation. Perkins knew what it was to scrape a potato from a village field by night, and more than once he was forced for some days to resort to weeds and dandelion roots.

As he went on excursions with Moir, Kerr and others, he saw at times scores of huge German troop-carrying planes passing over, heading for Libya; sometimes more than a hundred in one flight. This went on for weeks before Rommel made his big push. By night, the deep thrum-thrum of bombers penetrated the dark silence as they flew on missions to North Africa. The nights seemed endless, so that even these sounds were welcome as a stimulus to the imagination. There were no lights except the moon and the stars, and in the winter when the sun set the darkness settled over the island like a symbol of the Nazi oppression. The journeys that for safety reasons had to be made by night were haunted by the thought of walking into the arms of a German patrol or outpost, or of a mis-step on a narrow cliff path.

Cretans, too, needed to be wary of German deception. The Gestapo sent agents who spoke Greek into the mountains to pass themselves off as British evaders seeking help. To avoid getting caught in this well-baited trap Cretan villagers needed all their proverbial cunning.

Always there was the hope of escape. In October 1941, Dudley Perkins was with a group of between sixty and seventy evaders gathered around Elafonisi. For some time they watched the tantalising sweeps along the coast of a small, sleek Italian naval craft. As it moved close inshore they realised it was the sort of vessel they needed to take them to Egypt, not an open rowing-boat with makeshift sails. But so long as it kept to sea, not even the feverish imagination of the watching men could conceive a plan of piracy which would have a chance of success.

It was during this period that a Greek known as Captain George managed to interest some of the Cretan community in a proposal to buy a boat. Ned Nathan, a corporal in 28 Battalion, was one who was offered a chance of escaping.

The Torakis family — into which Nathan married after the war — subscribed a generous portion of the cost and Nathan's wife's cousin did much of the organising to collect the rest of the money in the villages (he later escaped to Egypt to join the merchant navy and survive two sinkings by enemy action).

George appears to have been a congenital liar, one who builds himself up as an important person, regardless of the truth and of the probability of being exposed. The Special Operations Executive in Cairo was organising rescue voyages for the soldiers known to be wandering free in Crete. British agents, landed at isolated spots by night, had made their way into the hills, contacting Allied Servicemen and arranging meeting places when boats were

58

expected — a motor torpedo boat, or launch or submarine. When the news circulated of Captain George's activities, it was assumed by some that he was an agent. Moir and Perkins were among those who received the whisper for a midnight rendezvous at a certain spot near Elafonisi. They found about twenty other New Zealanders waiting, but there was no sign of George and his boat. At daylight there was still no George. It seemed that the best they could do was split up, take cover, and wait for the next night.

The hopeful group waited through the afternoon. Once there was an alarm — movements in the bushes suggested that one party was being watched. After more such ominous movements the concealed men risked a challenge, and a Cretan cautiously showed himself.

With relief, Perkins and Moir recognised him. His name was Yiannis Glabadakis; he had been serving a fifteen-year sentence in Galatas prison and when it was bombed he had escaped. His conviction was for murder, apparently of three people. He was more anxious to escape from the island than the soldiers; if the Germans found him he would probably be shot out of hand, and if the relations of his victims caught him, he would certainly pay the penalty of the blood feud.

Later came a much more serious scare. Several German aircraft were heard and one seemed to be having engine trouble. It rapidly lost height and about 300 metres out to sea its nose dipped and it dived into the water — to the great delight of the watchers. The other aircraft circled above while two men in the wrecked plane climbed into a rubber dinghy and made for the shore. The planes overhead disappeared and soon a further aircraft arrived, made a landing on the beach, picked up the two men, and after a remarkably short take-off, flew away. As a climax to all this air activity a plane flew low over the area and dropped bundles of the same message distributed in other areas, calling on evaders to surrender!

Unbeknown to the larger group of men, a small party of five was in concealment further along the coast, including Nathan and the man who later became his cousin by marriage, together with two Greeks and a British soldier. Captain George was becoming alarmed as his passenger list grew, maintaining that if too many turned up at the rendezvous there would be trouble and the boat might be swamped. There had been heated wrangling over who had priority for departure on previous occasions, so his argument seemed sound. Nonetheless Nathan believed this to be all part of George's efforts to sustain confidence in himself and his plane.

So the two parties waited, and the second night passed without the appearance of George and his boat. Next morning the evaders scattered again, convinced that the Germans must have sighted some of them or were aware that they were in the area. Meantime John Kerr had discovered a boat on a beach some distance to the north in a little bay to the south of Mesara, a boat which he thought might be the one to be used by Captain George. It was certainly not worth the sum collected for its alleged purchase: it had no engine and appeared to be hardly seaworthy. They could only wait – and hope.

They had not heard the last of Captain George. Some time later word went round again that the would make an attempt to take off the men, this time from another bay near the one where Kerr had inspected the semi-derelict craft. By now his fame had spread and on this occasion there was a crowd of about fifty around the rendezvous, a dangerously large assembly. Very dubious about the whole affair, but still not without optimism, Perkins and Kerr were waiting and watching from a large cave high up on the slopes of a ravine overlooking the beach. From this vantage point they sighted two Germans moving round the rocks at the southern end of the bay. Others joined them and it was obvious that a large patrol was carrying out a methodical search, moving quietly without the usual rattle of small arms fire with which they sometimes combed an area.

Fortunately, the main group was searching southwards and only the two seen on the rocks at first were heading in the direction of the rendezvous. But as there was a chance that the hunt might swing back, and that some of the waiting men might run into ther Germans, Perkins and Kerr decided to create a diversion. Perkins had a hand grenade which he had taken from a German camp. They decided to toss it down a nearby ravine in the hope that it would explode, giving an alert to the hidden men and drawing off the soldiers. The grenade went off in the confined area with a crack like thunder, echoing along the valley for many seconds. Perkins and Kerr watched with satisfaction as the Germans withdrew from the bay and made for the village of Elos. It was clear they had received definite information that something was going on, for the patrol was a strong one, moving in trucks as close to the coast as was possible. Most significant was the presence of other, empty trucks, enough to transport a further fifty men! No more was heard of Captain George until Perkins and Kerr met him in June 1943, as related in the next chapter.

In contrast to George was a local man of a very different sort: Dimitrios Bidzenakis, of Roumata, known to many of the escaped soldiers as one of the bravest of their helpers. He gave shelter, food and guidance whenever he could, careless of personal sacrifice. A born fighting man, when a German patrol called at his village to make a periodical inspection, his first reaction was to go to his house, take out the machine-gun he kept hidden there and fire off a few rounds — just to make sure that it was in wokring order if it was needed. The subsequent scurry did not bother him at all.

The next attempt at escape by Perkins and Moir was in a four-metre boat taken from near the monastery of Chrisoskalitissas on the west coast. They sailed the craft south to Elafonisi and hid it while they collected stores and equipment, but the owners of the boat arrived and confronted the pair — almost apologetically —

after a successful exploration along the shore. The Cretans were quite amiable, understanding the plight of the soldiers, but they had their livelihood to consider. The only thing for Perkins and Moir to do was to hand over the boat with good grace, and the Cretans departed as friends. Moir later remarked that because of its size the boat would probably have been the death of them in an attempt to cross to Africa, so it was probably just as well their desperation was checked.

At about this time Perkins met the Paroulakis family of Langadas village in the Palekanos district. The family sheltered him for several weeks; particularly attentive were the two Paroulakis girls — Mary and Athena — who nursed him back to health and became his strong admirers.

After the war they settled in the United States; in a letter to New Zealand, Manos Paroulakis wrote of the 'enthusiastic and astonishing pleasure' he felt in communicating with Perkins' friends:

'We first met Dudley in September 1941 in distressing conditions and we kept him in our home until December. He did not know the language at first, but little by little we got to understand him.

'During his stay we shared the dangers and poverty during the German occupation. Many nights we slept in the branches of trees to save ourselves from falling into the hands of our enemy. While living with us Dudley was always a gentleman, and his great patriotism and heroism was often shown to us in very difficult times, and we, his comrades, and also our parents, learned to love him as if he was our brother and son, and he is to us now and for ever our brother.

'He always had it in mind to escape together with other soldiers who had great confidence in him and who looked to him as a leader. In November 1941 Dudley and four others made an effort to escape in a rowing boat. They brought the canvas sail off the boat and we mended it, and he bid us goodbye for the last time and he was on his way to Egypt as we thought . . .'

A short way out to sea they ran into rough weather and spent hours baling and rowing without making any progress before giving up and returning to shore. They tried again with a fishing boat they took from another beach. Under sail, the boat did not get very far before the wind dropped and it lay becalmed opposite a German guard post. The Germans apparently believed them to be fishermen and took no action. When a heavy swell developed and made everyone sick they also abandoned this attempt.

Quartered near Moustako, Perkins and Moir worked at times with R. W. Rolfe, a driver in the 4th Reserve Mechanical Transport Company, and Bert (H.W.) Gill, of 18 Battalion. They were 'billeted', as Rolfe puts it, in two homes in Vothiana with members of the Pontikakis family. Here Rolfe and Gill stayed for seven months. Even at this stage, after many had escaped by boat and the Germans were controlling or damaging the remaining craft, it was still possible to find the means to get away. Arriving on the west coast from time to time were boats that had been stolen, commandeered or purchased by members of the Cretan Division cut off in Albania when the Germans overran Greece. Some of these hardy men had refused to report to the enemy for deportation and found ways to return to Crete. Sometimes the cost of the boat that had brought a party from Greece would be recouped by selling it to British soldiers. It was certainly much easier for a Cretan to return home from mainland Greece than it was for a British soldier to attempt the journey to Egypt. Despite the risks, every wanderer dreamed of coming across a serviceable boat in a deserted spot.

Most of the returning Cretans landed on the north coast — it was nearer to Greece and the small Aegean islands could be used as stepping stones on the way. Some of the voyages, though not so protracted as that of Ulysses, took three or four months, as the party awaited suitable conditions for the next stage or repaired their craft.

Not all of these parties reached home. Apart from the usual hazards of the deep, they were likely to become blown off course or stray into minefields. Trying to find out where minefields were was one of the reasons fordelay in the stages from island to island.

Rolfe and Gill heard from Kerr of a boat near the lighthouse at Elafonisi, on the island they could reach by wading. Kerr had examined the craft and decided it was not fit for a long voyage and would require the work of several men to put it into shape. He was not optimistic about the chances even then and merely passed the information on to Gill and Rolfe for what it was worth. They in turn shared the discovery with Moir and Perkins and the four together made their own inspection. They believed that if the boat was submerged for about a week the planks would take up sufficiently to stop the leaks, and with a sail it should be seaworthy.

They then split up into separate missions. Gill and Rolf went back to Vothiana to get some blankets for the sail. When they returned they found that someone else had been active – possibly a German patrol – for there was a gaping hole in the side of the craft where two planks had been smashed. It fell to Rolfe to make the repairs, so back he went on another trek for hammer, saw and wood. With very inadequate equipment they repaired the damage. Eventually one stormy night Perkins and his three companions put out to sea. The wind was too strong for the improvised sail to be used. There was no rudder and only three oars, and with one of these Moir tried to steer.

They rowed out from the rocky coast with some difficulty and met the full blast of the storm about fifty metres from the shore. The boat started to take water fast. Gill, in spite of being very sick, stuck to one oar and Rolfe to the other. Perkins, who was also ill, never stopped baling. For nine hours they worked – only to remain in almost the same position, but still afloat.

At about 5 a.m. they managed to pull into a sandy cover a short distance from their starting point. The dinghy sank where they left it. From the beach they went up a hill to a little church where they all collapsed, and it was about twenty-four hours before any of them felt able to stir. After consulation, they decided that the boat was useless and returned to their villages until something else turned up.

This was a typical experience. They were probably lucky not to have cleared the island before trouble struck them, but such an enterprise must always have something of the foolhardy about it. Not only were there the hazards of the voyage, but the uncertainty of the landing. One party did make the Libyan coast safely, only to find that their landfall was behind the German lines!

Even seemingly sound, well-informed advice can have unfortunate repercussions. Captain Montague Woodhouse, who was with Freyberg when the 1941 battle began, was back in Crete as a secret agent; he advised a group of New Zealanders that they could be taken off by a submarine from Tris Ekklisies (Three Churches), along the coast to the east. To get there, he told them to head for the upland plain of Lasithi, which was in the eastern area under Italian occupation. While the Italians may have been less zealous, the Cretans in that region were neither as loyal nor as hospitable as their countrymen in the west. In due course the whole party was rounded up and treated as prisoners far more ignominiously than they would have been by the Germans. When Woodhouse visited New Zealand after the war, one of the men told him how the affair had ended. He was most concerned, having done what he thought was best at the time, and in his distress offered a totally unnecessary apology.

After the fruitless excitement around Elafonisi, Perkins and Moir trekked eastwards to investigate a rumour about British submarine activity. On their way they passed through the central region of the White Mountains where they found the Germans were carrying out a big drive to recapture escaped prisoners. They had boxed in the western part of the island and were moving towards the coast slowly and thoroughly. The two found themselves caught up in this drive without being aware of it and actually passed through the German lines twice, spending several days in the box. On one ocassion they encountered Germans unexpectedly and had to flee; the resulting escapade lasted all day. It began when they were machine-gunned from a range of only 200 metres. Miraculously, they were not hit and eight. Germans pursued them. For many hours they hid, ran, and hid. Only when night fell were they able to steal away to a safe distance from the patrol.

In another such incident, after resting in the sun with a flask of wine and feeling very much at ease, they got up and went on their way. Incautiously they crossed a ridge so that they were silhouetted against the sky. A burst of machine-gun fire from about 300 metres away made them dive smartly for cover. For the rest of that afternoon they played a strenuous game of hide-and-seek with the Germans. Again, darkness put an end to the pursuit. After this they passed once more through the German cordon and headed back to more familiar and, usually, less exciting territory.

Some soldiers were recaptured at this time while others, impressed by the coming winter and by German activity, did surrender. This worked in favour of those who remained at large for the Germans, apparently pleased by the result, or ignorant of the large numbers still at liberty, called off search operations for a while.

The next few weeks were comparatively peaceful and the more determined of the evaders were able to move freely about the island looking for a chance to get away. Later, the searches were renewed with vigour. The common practice was for an enemy troop to surround a village during the night and for the soldiers to go in at daybreak and search every house. (This was why Manos Paroulakis spent nights with Perkins in trees). By night, the villages would be empty of menfolk who preferred trees, caves or the better shelter of schools and chapels high in the hills to the risk of being dragged off to forced labour — or the possibility of being shot as a warning to others. Manoli Paterakis, of Koustoyérako, recalls that he helped Perkins to get a boat from a Cretan who was willing to let the New Zealander have it, but like many other attempts to sail away, this effort too was to prove unsuccessful.

FIVE

Illness, Celebration and Escape

Man's courage is the only true wealth;
Eat, drink and make the best of the world.

— Cretan *rizitika*

In the latter part of 1941 the stragglers derived much satisfaction from the continual waves of British aircraft flying overhead on their way to bomb Maleme airfield and shipping in Souda Bay. Whenever they appeared the men would watch enthralled and sometimes even jump for joy. Always the sight of the raiders gave them fresh hope that one day they would be free.

In November, Perkins found a boat lying high and dry on a beach. He and a friend planned to put it in the water and when the seams had filled to get away. But before they could launch it an Allied aircraft crashed on the beach; expecting it to attract the Germans they put the craft in the water immediately and set off. It leaked so badly it sank before they had gone very far, leaving them to swim back.

The plane was a British Bristol Beaufort, which had been photographing damage at Maleme after in RAF raid. It made its crash-landing near the northern end of the bay at Elafonisi, hitting the water first and then coming to rest on the beach. A German outpost was located on a headland immediately above, but because the plane was right under the slope the guards did not see it. Rolfe and Gill, risking detection, went to the plane and dragged the fir-men airmen out. The crew were all suffering from bruises and

68

minor injuries, including one or two sprained ankles. They were in no shape to travel very fast or very far.

Although the Germans were ignorant of the prize below, others were not. The injured men were assited inland by Cretans and evaders to the village near where Kerr was staying. The difficulty of the journey can be judged from the fact that while Kerr was able to cover the distance in three hours, the party with the sick men took three days.

There was another task to be carried out — salvaging the equipment and destruction of instruments and vital parts before the Germans made their inevitable discovery. In spells over four days this work continued with as little noise as possible.

When the gutted shell was found, the hunt was on for the missing airmen. They were regarded as being of much more importance than the stragglers from the army! News was somehow leaked to the Germans as to where the airmen were hidden. A surprise raid was made and the village surrounded. The first house the patrol entered contained one of the men and he was captured. The others managed to get away before the search reached the houses where they were staying.

During the subsequent excitement and undesirable presence of Germans, Kerr decided to shift camp. At one of the villages he again joined Moir, Gill and Rolfe. There was a rumour that special arrangements were being made to get the airmen out, and they were hoping to leave with them.

Towards the end of the year Perkins contracted jaundice and had to lie up for some time. He received some attention from the local barber — the link between barbers and surgeons is an old one — but it may be doubted if the treatment helped him very much, including as it did blood-letting from the scalp. During this time the others continued their hopeful expeditions. There was little enough reason for hope, however, as the winter was setting in and the normal risks of any escape attempt were greatly increased by the uncertainty of the weather. In fact, no New Zealanders escaped from Crete between November 1941 and April 1942.

The curtain rises once during this period when Perkins gives a glimpse of himself at a time when there was every reason for spirits to be at a low ebb.

'Christmas Eve', he worte, 'I spent in a stable alongside two pigs, a donkey, a couple of goats, three sheep and a few fowls — good company.

'I had a bout of jaundice and was about as yellow as a Chinaman.'

He was then in the village of Sklavopoula, among the highest and farthest west in the mountains. Ill though he was, he was among the guests invited to a Christmas party given by Fifi, wife of Dr Papantonakis, who was Chief Medical Officer for Crete and lived mainly in Chanea. The family was wealthy; their Sklavopoula home was large and comfortably furnished. Also in attendance were Ned Nathan and Jim McDevitt, who 'lodged' in one of the family's rooms. McDevitt remembers it as a very jolly gathering with Fifi's two younger sisters, Maro and Cleo, several local girls, and relatives of Fifi's husband. Ned and Jim stacked their beds and other furniture against the walls of their room and turned it into a 'cabaret' room with music from an ancient gramophone with a large trumpet for a speaker. Ned Nathan played a banjo, someone else played a mouth organ, and every-one joined in Boomps-a-Daisy and the Lambeth Walk, two dances popular in the western world at that time. This was the only time escapers danled with cretan girls or held them in their arms. Strict local customs prohibited such close contact.

Wine flowed plentifully and amongst the food the *pièce de résistance* was a cake, baked by Fifi, in which there was a single coin. Everyone had a share of the cake without anyone receiving the coin, until only one piece remained. It was decided that this should be the piece for the house, and since it obviously concealed the coin, must bring luck. McDevitt believes the luck held, for when the Germans raided the place many weeks later, he and others were able to escape in time without compromising the Papantonakis family. Much later, however, Fifi and her husband were betraved and were gaoled by the Germans.

Christmas for the British airmen from the crashed Bristol Beaufort was spent with Dimitrios Bidzenakis of Roumata, who had been sheltering them. They had an equally enjoyable time.

Fifi organised another party for New Year, when there was a heavy fall of snow. Dudley, Tom and John Kerr, little acquainted with snow, went outside to make snowballs. Soon the village girls joined them in a rollicking snow fight until exhaustion drove them indoors.

Tom Moir recalls on occasion when several German officers arrived at Fifi's house while he and Perkins were supping wine in an upstairs room. The Germans had trekked up the mountains from their camp several kilometres away and Fifi, always the perfect hostess, ushered the Germans into her ground floor rooms and served them food and drink. Moir and Perkins were concerned as much for the Papantonakis family as for their own safety. The two New Zealanders were in civilian clothing and, if discovered, the Germans would probably have shot them. Tragedy would almost certainly strike the Greeks — they would have their house burned to the ground and lose their own lives.

But Fifi carried on regardless, perfectly calm, reassuring Tom and Dudley that she could cope with the situation. She not only saw that food and more wine was provided for them, but she also managed to wheedle cigars from the Germans for her upstairs guests.

'The situation of our occupying the best rooms in the house and being supplied with cigars by the Germans downstairs was almost too much for the Greeks', said Moir. 'Their sense of humour came close to giving them away and the incident certainly caused great

71

general merriment after the Germans had left.'

Moir claims that Perkins' Cretan disguise at this time was so convincing that he was able to keep in with the Germans, 'who thought he was contra-British and pro-German. He was good to us and at the risk of his own life helped us many times.'

Kerr had come to Sklavopoula to see Perkins after learning about his illness. After staying a few days he suggested that the snow and the cold temperatures made life uncomfortable and they should seek warmer quarters down the mountains. It would be better, he said, for Perkins to return with him to Langadas, the village where he had formerly been, and where he had been well looked after. They thanked their hosts and moved on.

In the days that followed the conversation, as always, turned to the topic of escape. Kerr cherished for a time the thought of getting away in a German plane. He held a licence as a civilian pilot, and he spent some time scouting around an aerodrome. But his chance of flight from the island in this manner did not materialise. They agreed that too much loose talk had ruined many chances. The world would be passed round for days before an attempt, the party would grow too large, there would be lively farewells — all adding to the risks. The two men thus decided to work together in their own way.

Perkins' activities were still circumscribed by the after-effects of his illness. On some days his condition was normal; on others he was weak and listless. Describing their life at this time, Kerr claims that in all his experience with men he had never met anyone with such endurance under trying conditions as Perkins. Sometimes on the march Perkins would have to call a halt, but he would never complain. All he would say was: 'Isn't it funny, my legs have stopped working. Shall we have a smoke?' After ten minutes' spell, he would be itching to be on the way again. His independence drove him to do everything for himself — needlessly so, as on one occasion when he had woken up earlier than Kerr and feeling that a wash would refresh him, rather than disturb his companion or wait until he roused, he crawled to the stream two hundred metres away, and back.

On another occasion Kerr decided that they should halt outside a village instead of entering it, as he thought Perkins was unfit to go on. They found a hiding place some twelve metres down a steep slope from the path. The track here led over an overhang of rock and about halfway down this a tree jutted out which gave shelter and concealment. They spent the night there and in the morning went down to investigate the village. At the first house they met a Greek, known to them, who was there on a visit. They obtained information from him and were offered food, but as Perkins was fasting and needed rest he decided to go back to the shelter. Having discovered that another friendly Greek was in the next village, Kerr went on to see him.

It was about 6 p.m. when he returned, and he was shocked to find Perkins lying sprawled on his back in a clear space well down the rocks. He hurried down to find his companion torn and bloody. Perkins had lost all the skin off one side of his face, his nose had been bleeding freely, one trouser leg was ripped to shreds and the leg itself was torn and bleeding. Later Kerr found that almost all Perkins' body, especially down one side, was bruised where it was not grazed.

His friend was conscious though helpless. Looking up, he read the concern in Kerr's expression and commented: 'I'm a bit of a mess, aren't I?'

Just before reaching the point of the track above their hideout, Perkins had collapsed from fatigue and had lain where he fell. After some time — how long he did not know — he rallied sufficiently to realise his plight and understand that he must get off the track. He dragged himself to the rock edge and then he remembered nothing more until he was roused by Kerr's approach. Faint and giddy, he must have slid over the edge and fallen the twelve metres down the rough face.

This accident put an end to further travel for Perkins for some time. There was however one small compensation: his feet received much needed rest and attention. After his army boots had worn out he had been wearing a pair of German boots which he had bought in a village, but as they were too small they aggravated the blisters which had almost constantly troubled him.

During the period of convalescence two escape plans were being developed. Perkins and Kerr concentrated their efforts on a Cretan with whom an earlier contact had been made. He lived about halfway along the west coast and it seemed possible that he might be persuaded either to take his boat and go with them to Africa, or sell them the boat if they could raise the money. The latter could only be done by collecting it among the villagers, which would take time.

The response to the appeal for funds — it was not the first such collection to be made — was remarkable. Most of the money came through priests, but there were also a number of substantial gifts, including one from the Papantonakis family which had a high reputation for its generosity to British soldiers. The result was a sum of 380,000 drachmas. Because of wartime inflation it is impossible to give the sterling equivalent, but it was a sufficiently large sum to be a tempting bait for the purchase of a good-sized seagoing caique.

With this money Perkins and Kerr decided to drop out of sight of the villages, although Kerr would make occasional trips to one of the centres where the BBC radio news was available. He was also able to keep in touch with the movements of men whom they wished to accompany them on the escape.

All this was done with the greatest care. Inquires were made only in a general way, and when the time came it was intended that Kerr would tell the others simply that Perkins wanted to see them. No mention of a boat or an escape was to be made.

Their hideout at that time was in the hills overlooking the west coast; but their cave faced east with a view over a deep valley enfolding the villages of Vothiana and Moustako which were quite a brisk walk away. In Vothiana was a mill whose owner had given invaluable help to stragglers. When he made contact with Perkins and Kerr he refused to give his name in the interests of his own security, but he agreed to supply them with what food they needed on condition that they did not show themselves in the vicinity by daylight and did not come near the mill.

The precautions were not unreasonable: the cave was below a footpath leading to a cultivated area shared by three villages and two British soldiers moving about the area would be seen sooner or later by quite a number of people. They and the miller, therefore, would be in constant danger from an informer. The miller, or one of his family, was to take food up to the cave when convenient and bring information. Some New Zealanders knew the miller as Alex Makrakis.

The miller also made a substantial contribution to the fund for the boat. This effort, however, proved to be in vain. Despite the care which had been taken in making the collection, it was obvious that the purpose would be known to many. Among the many there must have been one careless or unreliable person or it may simply have been that by bad luck a German patrol visited the locality about the critical time. In any case, the boat owner with whom they had been negotiating became frightened and refused to have anything to do with the escape effort.

Moir and the others, who were living about twenty minutes' walk down the valley, were active in another direction. They had made contacts with a group in the north-west corner of the island near Mesara Bay, where a number of boats were held under German guard. These boats were kept under observation for some time and the movements of the guards carefully checked. They conceded that there was a considerable risk, but a party was formed which was confident that a successful attempt could be made to seize one of the boats. A date was set and Perkins and Kerr were informed of the rendezvous, but while they were waiting the pair decided to make one more endeavour to find someone who would sell them a boat. Once more they were unsuccessful.

The evening chosen for Moir's attempt was a dark, moonless one. The members of the party set out from their various hideouts and made their way to the beach through olive groves lining the flat stretch of land between the hills and the sea. It was so dark that some men lost their way; by the time they were all assembled, the night was too far spent for them to get a sufficient distance down the coast before dawn.

Perkins and Kerr had also made a start, but Perkins was still suffering from his illness and he was able to go only part of the way. Kerr continued and explored the bay thoroughly, although he thought that if an attempt had been made, it would have been carried out earlier in the evening. He saw and heard nothing so he went back to Perkins and they returned once more to their cave.

Moir and the others made another sortie the next night. This time they were successful. They broke into a boatshed and took the craft inside, risking detection by both German guards and the owners. Luckily the Germans did not discover Moir's enterprise, but the owners did. They confronted the escapers and there was argument — heated on the Cretans' side and accompanied by loud protestations — but the escapers were quietly determined. Fortunately the Cretans did not carry their objections to the point of betrayal. The boat was taken and later the stragglers still left on the island took up a collection of money to assuage the anger of the owners, who had the task of convincing the Germans they did not sell the boat or acquiesce in its theft.

Moir's group sailed some fifty kilometres towards the southwestern corner of the island. They sheltered in a cave near Elafonisi, its two-metre-wide entrance from the sea allowing the boat to be floated inside, hidden from prying eyes. The cavern led to the cliff-top with an exit through a small hole well concealed from casual view. During the next two days Moir made every effort to locate Perkins and Kerr. On the third day, reluctant though he was to leave them behind, when a favourable wind sprang up from the north-west he felt he could delay no longer and so put to sea.

There were eight in Moir's party, including Gill, Rolfe, two other New Zealanders, B. W. Johnson (5th Field Regiment) and G. G. Collins (20 Battalion), two Australians and a Royal Marine. Another New Zealander, Ken Little, was to have gone too, but he believed he would overload the boat and backed out. He escaped later.

Moir had had no previous sailing experience, and he had no compass, but he had some knowledge of the stars. Using them to steer his course, he kept steadily south. It was rather more than brisk sailing. The seas were rough, the wind strong but steady and they made good way. Several planes, Allied and German, flew overhead, but the conditions secured for them a certain immunity from molestation. They were not harassed and late afternoon on the fourth day they landed in North Africa on a small beach near Sidi Barrani. It was May 1942, nearly a year after the capitulation in Crete.

For his leadership in organising the escape, Staff Sergeant Tom Moir was awarded the Distinguished Conduct Medal. Lance Corporal Johnson received the Military Medal, and PrivateCollins was mentioned in despatches. News of the escape was eventually conveyed to Perkins and Kerr by their guardian miller. The full story of the misadventure was pieced together only when Perkins and Moir met later in Cairo. There was considerable hue and cry over the exploit, causing Perkins and Kerr to lie very low. After a fortnight they began once more to put out feelers. Fortunately Perkins was in better health and was able to undertake more strenuous excursions.

Upon reaching Cairo Moir had reported that many more men were in hiding in Crete, awaiting a chance to leave. Two naval craft were despatched within a month. On 25 May a fast motor-boat returned to Bardia with thirty-one rescued soldiers, including nine New Zealanders. A fortnight later, on 8 June, another lot with eight New Zealanders was brought back the same way. However none of the men in the west Selino area was among those then rescued.

The men in hiding placed great store in keeping abreast with the course of the war. This they did by listening to the BBC news from London on the few illicit radio sets owned by Cretans who ignored German edicts forbidding them to listen to British broadcasts.

One such secret radio was at the village of Kallithea, about five kilometres over the hills to the east of Vothiana. It was owned by George Fratzeskakis, whom Perkins visited on occasion. Much later, the Germans discovered the set. George was arrested by the Gestapo and he was sentenced to death for operating an illegal wireless. This was commuted in leniency measures to celebrate Hitler's birthday; instead he was sent to the notorious Auschwitz concentration camp in Poland. He was severely wounded in Allied bombing of the camp but survived the war to return to his wife Alcilriades.

In early June, Perkins and John Kerr met up again with Captain George, whom they had been expecting many weeks earlier. The man and his wife had sailed a caique from north-western Crete to the south-west; they suspected that Luftwaffe patrols were keeping an eye on it so they planned to move it to safer waters during the night. In the darkness the caique struck a submerged reef and took water rapidly. Those aboard were fortunate to escape with their lives. It was beached at the disused port of Stomiou, within sight of a German coast-watchers' post high above at Moni Chrisoskalitassas. The craft was too badly damaged to be easily repaired, and raised hopes were again displaced by despair.

Captain George did eventually leave the island, but he headed for Greece, not Egypt, and it was reported much later that he became a wealthy man in Athens through black marketeering with Greeks and Germans alike. George would be a bold man if he ever showed his face again in the villages of Western Crete.

On the night of 6 June three parties of the Special Boat Section of the Royal Marines landed in Crete near Cape Trikala with the task of destroying aircraft on the airfields at Maleme, Kastelli and Timbaki. They were met by Captain Tom Dunbabbin who briefed them.

Lieutenant David Sutherland and Corporal Riley found that there were no aircraft at Timbaki. At Maleme, Major Mike R. B. Kealy, Captain Allott and Sergeant Feebery decided they had no chance of entering because the airfield was too heavily guarded. It was completely surrounded by wire fences, at least one of which was electrified. Machine-gun posts and searchlights were installed at tactically well-chosen points all round. According to Major Kealy 'there were so many police dogs about that the place sounded like Crufts (British dog championships) on showday.'

The third party, Captain Duncan, CSM Barnes and Corporal Barr, together with two Greek guides, had conspicuous success at Kastelli. They marched by night, rested by day, and were ready for action by evening on 9 June. They slipped past two German sentries and reached the north-east dispersal area. There they placed bombs on parked aircraft and in six trucks. They also planted explosive charges in four bomb dumps, seven petrol and two oil storage areas. The men were still inside the airfield when the first of the explosion thundered; others followed and flames shot skyward. But in spite of frenzied German activity and searches the sabotage party made a safe getaway.

Seventy German soldiers died in the explosions and the Germans admitted they lost seven aircraft and that destruction included 210 drums of petrol, three bomb dumps and six trucks. The incident had unfortunate consequences: all the German guards and 17 Greek night watchmen were executed. Three days after the operation Captain Duncan's party reached their evacuation beach.

A few days later another raiding party, landed by the submarine Triton, attacked Heraklion airfield. Led by Captain The Right Honourable Earl George Jellicoe, the six men saw over 60 aircraft, mostly JU88s. The others in the party were four Frenchmen and a Greek guide, Lieutenant Costi. They placed bombs on 20 planes and on crates of aircraft engines, also on a number of trucks. To escape, they walked out of the main exit behind a dozen German ground staff. The Germans shot 60 Cretan hostages in reprisal for this raid.

The Papanicolis, returning from its mission, put ashore some of the commandos to find stragglers.

Cretans saw the commandos strolling in a village on 15 June. Warily, they made contact with some New Zealanders and told them that heavily armed Germans in British uniforms were about, looking for evaders. But when some New Zealanders saw the 'Germans' they recognised the uniforms and the men for what they really were. From the commandos stragglers learned of an evening rendezvous point and began making their way there. But Perkins did not know of the commandos' presence until much later.

On this day Perkins was in another village to hear the BBC radio news on a clandestine wireless. Kerr was away elsewhere on a food mission as several days had passed without supplies from the miller, who was known himself to be short of food. On his way back, Kerr met the miller who was hastening to the cave in a state of great excitement, calling loudly, all thoughts of secrecy abandoned.

All Kerr could make out at first was that 'English John' had come back. 'English John' was a tank sergeant, John Medley, of the 4th Queen's Own Hussars, whom they had previously known. Medley, a resourceful man, had escaped from Greece by rowing from Cape Matapan to Western Crete where he met and lived with several New Zealand stragglers. When the R.A.F. airmen crashed on the west coast Medley knew that the British authorities would give priority to recovering such valuable trained pilots. He stayed close to them and managed to leave the island when the motor launch Hedgehog arrived to evacuate the airmen form Tris Ekklisies in the spring of 1942.

Because Medley knew the terrain he was asked to return with the Papanicolis as a guide for the raiding parties. Medley had made a promise that he would return 'If I have to bring G.H.Q. Middle East back with me.' He had bome ashore from the submarine with portable canoes and food. The Papanicolis could not come in too close so the escapers were to use the canoes to go out to it by night.

Not only was the coast rugged and the seabed rough but the waters of the Mediterranean are very clear so that submarines were spotted comparatively easily. To avoid navigation dangers, and to give herself plenty of room to manoeuvre and depth to submerge, the *Papanicolis* had to keep well offshore.

At least one submarine had come to grief on such a rescue mission. It was spotted as it was putting out and was pursued by aircraft until it blundered into a minefield.

After the miller had been calmed to coherence, Kerr learned of the rendezvous. The site was a place about an hour and a half's walk away. No time was stated, but from the miller's excitement there seemed to be some urgency, and Kerr had no idea how old the news might be. There was no way he was going to leave without Perkins and he hurried off to find him.

Kerr's hunt for Perkins, racing across tussocky countryside to places where he might be, took several hours. It was three in the afternoon when he came upon Perkins and, in great excitement, they hurried off to collect their belongings from their cave. By the time they had returned to the point where Kerr had me the miller another three hours had passed. So, as so much time had been lost, they decided not to go back to the cave, but to abandon their scanty possessions, including a diary Perkins had been keeping, and to head for an area they knew as Mesara Bay, on the west coast.

Anxious not to miss this chance of escape, they took the risk of going by the shortest route, which involved going along a beach in full view of a German guard post. At a distance there was nothing to distinguish them from Cretans — their clothes were made up of odds and ends and even the wearing of army garments attracted no special notice by this time. And they had magnificent Cretan *moustachios*.

The risk, the excitement, the rapid journey were all a strain. As they plodded on the excitement died, the thought of danger receded. There was left only dogged determination: there was not even hope, there had been too many disappointments in the past. As the last light drained from the sky they reached the rendezvous, and sure enough 'English John' was there.

Medley told them the submarine was due in later that night. Some escapers were being taken off elsewhere and, if the submarine had sunk any vessels during its mission to Crete, there might well be survivors aboard. In that case there might be little room to take on more people. There was thus no certainly that Perkins and Kerr would get away. This confirmed the skinking feeling the two had experienced on the journey — they were the last to arrive among the waiting group.

It was late when the submarine signalled from well offshore. There was a heavy sea running and the English captain was being more cautious than usual as his craft had been sighted during the afternoon and attacked with depth charges. There was also a possi-

82

bility that a night patrol might sweep some of the bays and use flares. The first commando canoe put out with a handful of men and disappeared into the darkness. There was an anxious wait — so long that the men on shore began to fear that something had happened. Then the sumbarine's dinghy came in with two crew. Unless conditions improved, they said, no more men could be taken aboard that night. If possible, another attempt would be made on the next.

The hopes of Perkins and Kerr sank — they had been unlucky once again. They sat on the rocks, exhausted and depressed. They were about to move further back from the shore to find a sheltered place and settle down to sleep when they heard the splash of oars. Apprehensively, they waited. It was the dinghy. Apparently the captain had decided to make another trip.

Almost from the outset the attempt seemed doomed. As the boat lay alongside the rocks a sudden wave heaved up, the dinghy hit a projection and one of the planks at the stern was holed. Water poured in, steadily filling the boat until Perkins took off one of his German knee boots and rammed it into the hole. With the other he baled and gradually made the boat sufficiently buoyant to put off. Kerr and one sailor took the oars while Perkins and the other took turns at baling. This had to be kept up all the way, for the dinghy was shipping water in addition to that still coming in through the plugged leak. A hundred metres, two hundred metres were laboriously covered — and then they sighted the submarines slowly moving away. The captain had evidently given up for the night.

All four yelled, and yelled again. As they watched they saw the long shape slowly start to turn and circle back towards them.

There was another tricky operation yet to be managed. They were hailed from the submarine and told to abandon the dinghy. Four ropes were flung when the submarine got close and each man was to grab one and hold on. There was no time for argument for the dinghy was already sinking. The four men were in the water, naked and swimming, when the ropes reached them. Clinging desperately, they were hauled in and lugged up the sides with water pouring from them. Immediately they were shoved down the hatchway, as unceremoniously as fish being tossed into a trawler's hold.

Straight away the hatch was down and the submarine was below the surface. There was no time to be lost. They had to get well out before dawn — which was then not far off — and before the reconnaissance planes put out on their morning sweeps. The submarine also had its own patrol to complete.

As day broke, the *Papanicolis* cruised along the west coast and stayed for some time off the south-west corner of the island. Later, its mission completed, the submarine headed for Alexandria. Aboard were eight New Zealanders among the stragglers rescued on this occasion.

For Perkins and Kerr it was a strange, confused awakening. Around them were the riveted steel sides of the submarine instead of the limestone sides of the cave, and the air was warm, almost hot, and heavy with the smell of oil. As they lay, they could feel themselves roll first to one side and then the other as the submarine changed course. There came a heavy thump . . . another . . . and another, each less violent than the last. Clothing and other objects hanging round the walls swung out and then fell back. Small objects rattled to the floor.

Then came a fourth concussion, but no more. The submarine held to a steady course, tilted slightly as she sought greater depth and levelled off. The engines stopped. Officers came through to reassure their passengers. The submarine had been spotted from the air and depth charges had been dropped. Now the craft would stay immobile where it was until the roving planes above gave up the hunt and flew away.

Time passed without the submarine making any move. Over-

84

head the planes persisted in their search. Eventually the thump of depth charges was heard and felt again. Perhaps some oil, or a change in the angle of the light, had revealed her shape to watching eyes?

There were several such incidents during the day, all uncomfortable, especially for the soldiers who were in a completely strange environment and one which they did not wholly trust. They were, too, in an abnormal state, weakened physically and their nerves strained by months of hardship. After finally escaping from their prison island, they were now lying helpless, fathoms deep, in a stell container which shook from time to time as high explosives sought to destroy it.

Late that day, when it was safe to move, the submarine got under way and off the island of Gavdos she hove to for the night. Next morning, as the craft continued the journey to Egypt, the aerial patrol became active again, dropping bombs which fell wide. For the passengers, uneasiness gave way to boredom and impatience until reaction set in and they surrendered to their exhaustion. After some hours, when all had been quiet for a long period, the captain took the craft up to periscope depth to look around. The area seemed clear, so he risked breaking surface and opened the hatch. Immediately he pulled it closed again with a clang and the roar of an aeroplane engine could be heard overhead. The alarms sounded as the submarine went into an emergency dive.

It was a steep, fast dive, so precipitate that the vessel was at maximum depth before the forward tanks filled; weighed down by the weight behind she was unable to level off. Instead, she moved from the forward diving angle into a reverse position, almost perpendicular. For the passengers, who did not know the extent of the danger, it was a peculiar experience. They suspected the worst as they looked down the passageway, stretching almost like a well below them as they clung on. They could see the crew Half English, Half Greek, frozen at their posts. Gradually, the craft righted itself. By that time some of the crew had to be freed from the controls, their muscles cramped into rigidity. One degree more, said the captain later, and the ship would have become unmanageable, tilting further and further and plunging to the depths with machinery tearing loose and crashing through the steel skin.

The long spell of inaction that followed this experience was welcome. At night a radio message broughts some more excitement — a warning that the Italian fleet was being forced out to sea. The Greek submarine was ordered to proceed at full speed and stand by at a given spot. There was much to be done in the way of preparing for action. The crew's ordered movements were busier than usual and a feeling of excitement mounted in tune to the hum of the diesels.

Anti-climax. By the time the submarine arrived the clash was over. The craft was well off course now and further away from Alexandria. Supplies were running low. It was home this time, or not at all.

Alexandria looked much better to the returning men than it did when they had left it a whole lifetime previously. The submarine pulled in alongside they Navy's flagship where they were made welcome. They relished their first hot bath for months, were given a big breakfast, cigarettes and a patriotic parcel. Then they were summoned to an interview with Admiral Cunningham, Perkins still sporting a beard and moustache in the Cretan style.

It was the time of German successes in the desert and the enemy had encroached to the outskirts of Mersa Matruh in an attempt to press forward to Cairo. In Alexandria, the Navy was engaged in preparing for defence and possible withdrawal should the need arise. On shore at last, the men were taken over by the army which issued new clothing and put them in barracks with strict instructions to be silent about where they had been and what they had seen. For two days Navy Intelligence officers questioned them meticulously on every detail of their time on Crete. The interrogations were interspersed with visits to town, money in advance of pay and medical checkups. A naval boat was made available for trips on the harbour. After Intelligence had finished with them, the Air Force went through the whole interrogation procedure again.

Letters home supplementing the official cables sent to parents and subject of course to censorship were not permitted to reveal much about what what had occurred in the long period since they had sailed for Greece. The stories they would like to have told would have to wait. In Cairo, at the headquarters of the Allied Forces in the Middle East, Army Intelligence took them through their whole story once more. Although the Army had the dossier from the Navy it had its own interests. So it all came out again — names, places, dates, hiding places, movements, beaches, garrison points, friends and suspects. Perkins and Kerr still had the 380,000 drachmas collected to buy a boat. This they handed over` on condition that it would be used for relief work in Crete. Had they not escaped by submarine it is probable this sum would have secured the type of craft necesary to reach Egypt safely.

From Cairo they went to the base camp at Maadi, to the south of the city, and were offered home leave. Both were reluctant to take it. Although still weak from his ordeal in Crete, Perkins knew that if he returned to New Zealand he might be retained there on training duties. He had volunteered to fight the war and he felt circumstances had prevented him from doing very much. He had a fortnight's leave and by the middle of July he was back with his unit in the desert.

Kerr sought a posting to Headquarters, Army Service Corps, but was denied this. Dissatisfied with this decision, he took off from Maadi and hitchhiked to El Alamein where his unit of the ASC was stationed. He was lucky that his colonel took the best view of his indiscretion and set matters to rights with a signal back to base.

Kerr served with the Eighth Army all the way to Gabes Cap and there he was recalled for New Zealand furlough. Wishing instead to go to England, he changed his next-of-kin, giving an English address. While there he engineered a transfer to RAF Bomber Command, using his civilian pilot's licence as a qualification.

After the war he returned to New Zealand, having completely lost touch with his former associates and not knowing of the fate of Dudley Perkins. He discovered this only later, through a newspaper article in 1951.

Woe, let nobody suffer my pains
Not a ship on the beach nor a bird in the plains.

— Cretan *mantinade*

SIX

Dynamo on Wire Legs

Fate, I don't fear you now, whatever you want to do to me,
If you have other torments I'm right here, come to me.

— Cretan *mantinade*

Perkins had been back with his unit only a few days when he was promoted to lance-bombardier on 20 July 1942. The 4th Field Regiment was not the same outift he had known before. He felt himself to be almost a stranger: he was ignorant of the full story of the losses in Greece and Crete, and the Division had been in some hard actions during his absence. The toll of war and the influx of reinforcements, in the ranks and among the officers, made the regiment almost a new formation with only a sprinkling of old hands. Nor was it the happiest of times to be joining a divisional unit. Rommel was driving towards Alexandria; the Eight Army was in retreat. The troops' confidence was undermined and morale had suffered.

For the next few weeks Perkins was swallowed up in the tide of events. He met old friends from time to time, and at El Hamman, where the Division was resting, an officer cousin, Captain Jim Bain, visited him. Subsequently they spent several pleasant evenings in conversation among the sandhills with Perkins recounting his adventures in Crete. About this time there was a reorganisation within the regiment and he became observation post assistant to the E Troop commander, Captain Richard Dyson, as part of 46 Battery. This was his role when the unit took part in skirmishes at

Munassib Depression and at Ruweisat Ridge. A fresh breeze was sweeping across the desert in the form of the new Commander-in-Chief of the Eighth Army, Lieutenant-General Bernard Montgomery, moving among the forces to see for himself what kind of fighting men they were. Montgomery was unfamiliar with the easy-going manner and laxer discipline among New Zealand and Australian servicemen. After a visit to the New Zealand Division Montgomery is reported to have complained to General Freyberg that very few of the men saluted him as he drove through the New Zealand positions. Freyberg, so the story goes, is said to have told Montgomery that had he waved the troops would have waved back.

To any observer it was obvious that a major battle was about to be fought, but Perkins was not to be in it.

Impressed with Perkins' abilities, Captain Dyson recommended him for an Officer Training Course. On 20 October, only three days before the beginning of the battle of El Alamein and now a full Bombardier, Perkins was one of a group which was pulled out of various regiments and sent to Maadi to the School of Instruction, there to prepare for an Officer Cadet Training Unit course in Palestine. Although rank meant nothing in an OCTU, a delayed promotion caught up with him and he became a sergeant.

While in Maadi, Perkins received news of Tom Moir, with whom he had previously exchanged stories of the misadventures at the time of the escape. Moir had been seconded to the British Special Operations Executive and was in training for a return to Crete. The two men met in Cairo and Moir disclosed in confidence what he was doing. He had been given permission to take someone to Crete, and the only person he would have considered was Perkins. The idea appealed strongly to Perkins, partly because of the free life, and partly because he was conscious of his debt to the Cretans. Moir, however, felt obliged to dissuade him. If Perkins went with him he would forfeit his opportunity to become an officer. Perkins was willing, but Moir thought that some day he might regret it so decided to go alone. It was, he comments, a decision with significant consequences for them both. Had they got together again their partnership might have meant better luck all round.

Then out of the blue, Perkins was 'returned to unit' from the OCTU course not long before Moir sailed to Crete — an indication that he had not been found satisfactory. Captain Dyson was appalled by the decision: there could be many reasons why a cadet might be dropped — and they were not always good ones. What had happened was this. One day, either in the mess or in a bar or restaurant, someone who also knew Moir began talking about his secret mission. Loose talk of this nature could endanger not only Moir but the work of the whole branch to which he was attached, as well as those he would be trying to help. Perkins protested, an action which was resented. There were further words, ending in a fight. This in itself would have been sufficient reason for a rejection from OCTU, although Perkins did not speak of it.

An OCTU course in the Middle East was always an ordeal. The cadets were under officers and NCOs from Britain, Australia and South Africa, as well as from New Zealand. The standard required in personell deportment and training was high, but discipline was often thought to be too rigid and unimaginative. The atmosphere of the unit, in field works as well as in lectures and even off duty, was apt to irk men accustomed to a much freer tradition. Instructors encouraged the asking of questions at the end of lectures, even though cadets probably already knew the answers. Keenness was apt to be judged by the number of questions asked, and to some this seemed puerile. It also encouraged something of a toadying spirit — there were, of course, army expressions for this — and such behaviour was always regarded by the New Zealanders as the lowest of the low. It seemed that the label 'lacks initiative' was attached to persons who failed to ask a question or two at question time; even more summary was the comment on anyone who asked the wrong sort of question.

In Perkins' case, to say he lacked initiative was patently absurd. He had already proved himself in Greece, in Crete and in the regiment. The truth of his 'failure' to gain a commission appears to be that he simply walked out of the course, having had enough of the way it was conducted. He left Palestine and arrived back at base in Maadi without a posting, technically absent without leave from OCTU.

Adjutant at the School of Instruction in Maadi at that time was the cousin Perkins had earlier met. Perkins' arrival posed a minor problem for Jim Bain in that he was on nobody's ration strength. Somehow Bain managed to put things right, having Perkins properly transferred in order, so that the record 'returned to unit' was made subsequent to his walkout and without any serious repercussions. General Freyberg took exception to the practice of OCTU returning men he had recommended for commisions. He was known to send back to OCTU rejected men with the instruction 'I did not send these men to you to be examined, I sent them to you to be trained as officer's — a comment which evidently referred to the attitude of some of the British officers running the unit.

In mid-January, Perkins was joined in Maadi by other returned cadets — 'nobody's babies', as one expressed it. Two were tent-mates of Perkins and another was later commissioned in the field. One by one they returned to their units, but Perkins remained. For him the decisive moment was approaching. His thoughts turned increasingly to the offer Moir had made. In Maadi, too, the presence of Greek soldiers reminded him of his Cretan friends, and soon he was meeting Cretan guerrillas who had been sent to Maadi for training in guerrilla warfare and sabotage. Talking with them in their own language, he felt he would like nothing better than to be able to be in Crete beside them. He also got to know some of the British officers in the Special Operations Executive.

In February Moir went back to Crete by motor-launch and on 18 March Perkins was marched into Headquarters, Middle East, for 'special duty', although remaining 'for all purposes' with the Army School of Instruction. He was now with S.O.E., and according to New Zealand Army records he was officially 'transferred to Force 133' on 28 April 1943.

S.O.E.'s work in Crete, begun soon after the 1941 battle, had developed into a comprehensive activity. Moir's task was to organise escapes and undertake sabotage. He knew several places where there were pockets of escapees still holding out and, knowing the men too, he had the best opportunity of seeking contacts with them. There were branches of S.O.E. in different parts of the island, and there were some very interesting characters among the members, most of them from the British forces. They were all volunteers and all had their own motives for undertaking the work. Some did it because they knew Greece, ancient and modern, and felt a special attachment to the Greek cause.

Thus it was that one day, Tom Dunbabin, a Greek scholar and a Fellow of All Souls College, Oxford, black-bearded and looking neither like a scholar nor a colonel in his Majesty's forces, sat in a very uncomfortable hill cave in Crete, gazing out at the dismal weather, and arguing with a very independent-minded New Zealander, Tom Moir, who had his own ideas about what he was going to do and how he was going to do it. Possibly Dunbabin acknowledged that Moir might have some knowledge of the matter. But when the discussions moved to other subjects on which Moir's views were equally definite, the older man may have felt that guerrilla warfare had brought him into contact with some very peculiar fellows. In the end, though, each had respect for the other. There was a lot of individuality in the S.O.E. Some of these men found regimental life confining and frustating. They were the sort of English who make remarkable solo journeys of exploration, who live for months with isolated native peoples, gaining knowledge of their ways and producing extraordinary books. They are the kind of men to whom war sometimes gives great opportunity, men such

93

as Lawrence of Arabia and Wingate.

Moir roamed extensively, mostly in the western area which was then under Major Xan Fielding's command. He sheltered at times with various families and the Germans got to know of the activities of an Englishman seeking out stragglers. Moir has not spoken of his time in Crete; possibly because there were incidents he preferred to forget. His eldest son, Dudley — named by Moir because of his respect for Dudley Perkins — confirms a story of German bestiality which his father witnessed through a crack while in concealment in a family's house. The Germans had called at the house, seeking 'the Englishman, Tom'. They demanded to know where he was and threatened to shoot every member of the family until they revealed his whereabouts. Fortunately, most of the members of the family had managed to get away earlier; only about three remained. The Germans first shot one and again demanded an answer and, when it was not forthcoming, shot another and later a third. One can only imagine Moir's thoughts and his conscience on the matter. But he knew that if he did reveal himself he would not have saved his benefactors, since the Germans usually shot out of hand anyone found harbouring wanted men. By staying put he probably saved the other members of the family from being hunted down.

On one occasion Moir spent two days with Fielding who remembers him as 'a staff-sergeant, a dark, silent man, so unassuming that to my shame I have forgotten his name'.

In two months Moir rounded up fifty-one men, fourteen of them New Zealanders. To begin with they were kept apart and only when arrangements were completed for their departure were they brought to a pleasant glade known as Koukonara, near Koustoyérako. There local villagers provided food and clothing. Among those hoping to get away was a crippled Australian who would need to travel from the Apokoronas region to Selino on donkeyback and under escort in case German patrols were encountered.

Anti-escaper activity was very lively at this time; all travellers on or near bypaths were stopped, questioned and searched. With the risk so great, no escort could be found for the task and the Australian had to be left behind, later to be found by Germans after being cared for by the Lagonikakis family in Neo Choria and hidden in a cave for about two and a half years.

While awaiting the evacuation Moir went off on a last reconnaissance to the northern side of the island, meeting misfortune on his way back. He had successfully accomplished a spying mission to the airfielf at Maleme and the port at Souda Bay to gather information for a commando raid planned over the next few weeks. Returning tired, he had crossed the mountains into Selino and was refreshing himself, along with an RAF interpreter who had accompanied him, at the fountain in the village of Moni. Here, he was approached by a German patrol which included a traitor known as Christos. The Germans were ready to accept Moir as a Cretan, which he appeared to be, but Christos was not fooled by Moir's Greek and told the Germans they should arrest him. Somehow Moir managed to slip his revolver and maps to a friendly Cretan, but when his nationality was established he was treated as a spy for being in civilian clothes.

Attempts were made to get the people of Koustoyerako, about eight kilometres from Moni, to rescue Moir before he was taken off to the dreaded Ayia gaol, near Galatas. They decided how-ever that if they did so it might jeopardise the safety of the fifty-one men nearby who were about to be evacuated. In the inevitable interrogations Moir insisted he had been a straggler on the island for two years. He never wavered from his story and in the end he was able to convince the Germans that this was the truth. After that he was accorded the usual treatment for a prisoner of war.

In Ayia gaol were Dick Huston and C. J. Ratcliffe, of 19 Battalion, and Lance-Sergeant G. M. Davis, of Divisional Signals. They had been caught in a cave before Moir could contact them, but three others in nearby caves, not discovered by the Germans, got away with the group Moir organised. These had all been two years in the mountains, helped by people in the foothills village of Varypetron. One particular house they visited was on the southern edge of the village and sometimes they slept there — much later the house was blown up by the Germans.

'Day after day they interrogated me,' said Dick Huston, 'trying to find out who sheltered and fed me. I kept saying, no-one. I wasn't going to tell.'

Once he was put before a firing squad and blindfolded. He thought his last moments had come, but it was only an attempt to try to get him to talk. Then he was told he would be handed over to the Gestapo, noted for their confessions gained by torture, but nothing happened.

Hostages taken from villages and farmhouses were housed in the prison. Some mornings cell doors would clang about 4 a.m. and unfortunates would be told it was their turn to die in revenge for the killing of a German soldier. In the grey dawn there would be a rat-rat-rat of machine-guns. When he saw the execution yard Dick thought it strange that the wall was pocked only a foot or two above the ground. Later he learned that the condemned were shot sitting down.

Dick Huston's sojourn in Crete ended when his captors sent him to Germany to spend the rest of he war in a prison camp. Moir also was eventually sent to Germany. Although he twice escaped in Europe, both times he was recaptured.

Jim McDevitti, meanwhile, was in hiding in Koustoyérako. Moir had arranged with him and another man to round up the members of the party still in surrounding districts. When the appointed time came and Moir did not appear, McDevitt and his companion became alarmed and decided to waste no more time in carrying out their part of the arrangements. What added to their uneasiness was the fact that the Germans were engaged in 'manoeuvres' in the Selino valley, where rifle and machine-gun fire could be heard continously. When it became known that Moir had been captured, Xan Fielding assumed responsibility for seeing the operation through. The party moved down to Tripiti, and there, on 9 May, they embarked on a Royal Navy ship for a safe journey to freedom. For his work on this operation Moir received the Military Medal to add to the Distinguished Conduct Medal he was awarded for his earlier determination in evading capture.

While Moir was busy in Crete, Perkins became acquainted with Rustom Building in Sharia Kasr el-Aini — a block of requisitioned flats close by the Garden City diplomatic quarter in Cairo — where S.O.E. had its headquarters. That the building was an intelligence centre appeared to be common knowledge in Cairo. Ask a ataxi-driver to go there and he would say: 'Aiwa, Secrets House!' Perkin's new masters in 'The Firm' — as agents referred to their organisation — sent him to Palestine for a course in guerrilla warfare. It was run from a requistioned monastery on the top of Mount Carmel and commanded superb views over Haifa and across the Bay of Acre to the north. The men knew it as Narkover — the name used by 'Beachcomber' for the school he wrote about in his *Daily Express* column.

Shortly before Dudley arrived, the establishment was the target of a daring raid by the Jewish Agency. The security guards were Jews and they allowed two military three-ton lorries containing men in uniform to drive into the camp. The intruders broke into the armoury, loaded thirty machine-guns and other arms onto the lorries and drove off, taking not only the guards but also the security officer, who himself was a Jew. The arms were used by the Jewish Agency for their underground forces and the commandant had to face a court-martial.

Work at the course was strenuous. The men were up at dawn, doing physical training. A Polish officer, Stas Lazarowicz, taught them the intricacies of enemy weapons. The trainees also studied uniforms, insignia, German and Italian badges, map reading, explosives, the art of demolition, secret inks, tapping telephone lines, lock picking and safe blowing. To help men endure the rigours of mountain warfare there wereunarmed combat classes and a weekly cross-country run. The only recreation was an occasional visit to the seaside for swimming.

On the same course was Captain Sandy (A.M.) Rendel, of S.O.E., who was receiving similar training prior to a posting in Crete, and was later conducting officer for Perkins' voyage. Knowing that Perkins had already been in Crete and knew something of the people and the island, Rendel struck up a friendship with the New Zealander, attracted by the great seriousness with which Perkins was taking the course. 'On the march,' he said, 'he looked like a fox-terrier quivering with eagerness.' Rendel learned much from Perkins about what to expect when he reached Crete, and he was impressed by the determination which the New Zealander displayed about returning in spite of his year of hardship, making light of the hazards to be encountered.

'He told me that he had not passed an officer's selection test and said, rather grimly, and I think because his feelings had been hurt, that it was allegedly for lack of the qualities of leadership. If so, this was, in my opinion, a great mistake. He had great qualities of drive and discipline, and (later in the year) his party in the hills, although I never saw them, was said to be under tight control. He carriee out, for instance, arms inspections and the Cretans were said to like it, although nothing could have been more ragged and irregular than the ordinary Cretan shepherd boys.

'When we first met on the course in Haifa, I picked him out, in my own mind, as a good man to work with. I was very keen myself on the course and it was obvious that among a good many others, some of whom were taking the whole thing as a light-hearted adventure, Kiwi, as everyone called him, was going to try extremely hard.

'We went on long walks together. One was a night march which took about four hours. He led at a smart pace all the way, and never missed his track, so that we won the competition with two or three hours to spare. The last hour was more of less a silent race between us. Both of us were determined, I think, to go really hard and not to ask the other to slow up. I think Kiwi was surprised, however, to find anyone who could stick to him. He was like an electric dynamo on wire legs.'

Later they went on another exercise, a voluntary one extending over a weekend in preparation for a five-day test at the end of the course. The trip took them across the hills to the Sea of Galilee, in hot weather. It was a tiring excursion which left both men in an irritable mood, but Rendel's respect for Perkins continued to increase.

'He was completely confident that he would overcome any difficulties about the life in Crete, and this helped me a lot in prospect of what was to come. He told me something of the time he had spent in Crete after the battle, going from place to place with his friend, Moir. He said he had been chased for about five days, once, during a German exercise. But he did not seem to regard it as a particularly grim experience, nor to have suffered from lack of food.

'I asked him if he would join my party in Crete, and he said he would be ready to, but thought he would be sent to Selino in the West because he knew that region best. This, in fact, happened (I was going to Eastern Crete). I think he would, in any case, have wanted to lead his own party.'

Then came the five-day exercise. They started out with a reconnaissance of a power station and then made a very hot walk up the Jordan valley. They walked most of the following night and reached the midway rendezvous at midday the next day, where they rested till nightfall and then in company with some other pairs carried out a sabotage exercise, blowing up iron girders in a gully.

They walked through the night and next day passed through several Arab villages:

'We were by then rather tired. I felt Kiwi was a touch scornful when I bought some food. He thought we still had plenty — and he was quite right — and that anyway he had brought too much and thus we had too much to carry, and that it would have been better to have tested ourselves without food. He was, in fact, more Spartan about in than the test prescribed.'

During the day Perkins developed trouble with his boots and suffered a sore hell, but it made no difference to his determination to go on. From this point, though, the test became an ordeal which reached a climax after Rendel in turn raised a blister on the ball of one foot. The suppressed fellings eventually blew up into a row in which the New Zealander became very heated and the Englishman somewhat cold. The consequence was they both settled down to slog out the rest of the march as fast as they could.

'When we got to our next halt,' Rendel goes on, 'we were still in effect not on speaking terms, and I wanted to end that and panted out the time of the last stage — over six kilometres in about forty-five minutes — and added that to make really good progress, the remedy seemed to be to have a row.

'Kiwi gave a mixture of snort and laugh, and added, I remember, to my astonishment: "That's the trouble with you British. One can never get the better of you. You always keep your temper!"

The last part of the test was the approach by night up a steep mule path to a certain house, passing it without raising an alarm. Here, for the first and last time, to Rendel's knowledge, Perkins missed his way, thus adding some distance to their journey. Despite the coolness that still remained between them, Perkins acknowledged his error and apologised — an act for which Rendel gave him full marks. The exercise was to end in deep disappointment, however, when they were spotted trying to get near the house.

There are some final impressions from Rendel: 'At the end of the course, he must have been trained absolutely to the last muscle. He looked brown, rather slight, but lean and fit. I don't think he was interested in the end-of-course jollifications. I don't remember him ever relaxing over a drink but he never gave the impression of being a spoilsport and he seemed to have exceptional self-discipline which certainly commanded respect from all of us.'

From Haifa the trainees went back to the villa in Sharia Asmoun, Heliopolis, which was the mission mess. They were there for some weeks, marching to keep fit and attending to quartermastering requirements for equipment. Dunbabin visited the mess on leave from Crete; he told Perkins that his former companion, Moir, had been picked up by the Germans, and that his fate was unknown. It must have been a heavy blow, but Dunbabin noted that Perkins appeared absolutely unshaken.

It seems evident that while the earlier months on Crete had been a time of preparation, aim and purpose had not been consolidated for Perkins until the shock of his epxerience at the officers' course. After he had rallied from that blow, Perkins was single-minded, dedicated to what he saw to be his task. He also had to prove himself. It was not that he sought distinction: he had to do a good job in order to live with himself, and with others.

When Perkins told Rendel how he had sometimes dug up Cretan potato patches by night to survive, Rendel says he could scarcely believe Perkins would stoop to thieving since 'he was such a virtuous young man.' Such food was stolen only from Cretans who were known to be more sympathetic to the Germans than to the resistance, or were active collaborators; but back on the island in 1943 the need to forage for food no longer existed. With him on the journey from Cairo had come substantial food-stocks and Fielding, in command at the camp near Koustoyérako, had been able to organise adequate supplies from local sources which were to be supplemented by airdrops.

SEVEN
The Guerilla Hideout

He must not step on Cretan earth who's not a brave man.
On Cretan earth must only step in weapons, a craftsman.

— Cretan *mantinade*

At Kaloyeros and along the coast, where Perkins and George Psychoundakis had landed, ravine-riddled mountains tower high
overhead. As Perkins already knew, there were no roads, only
mountain trails trodden by goats and shepherds. With the departure of the donkeys carrying the stores and equipment, the men
remaining at Kaloyeros had only their own *sakoulis* to shoulder.
One of the younger Cretans — many of the youths regarded Psychoundakis as a kind of hero — offered to carry the homecomer's
haversack. This left Psychoundakis with only a light load. Fielding,
lugging the heavy haversack of gold, recalls thinking how riches
can be a burden; perceiving George without his *sakouli* he asked
him to take the heavy bag, adding laconically, 'It's very light.' On
this, his second day back in Crete, Psychoundakis had not yet got
back into form for long-distance walking and hefting a heavy pack
on a steep climb, in spite of trying to keep fit by running up the
Pyramids. He fell so far behind that Andonis Paterakis was sent
back to look for him. Andonis found George resting; he swung the
haversack onto his shoulders, and when they had caught up with
the others Psychoundakis told Fielding: 'You take your nice light
sakouli and let's see how far you get with it!' Fielding had had his
little joke and took the bag.

A reminder of the German presence was a rocky mound and four wooden crosses where enemy soldiers had executed Cretans whom they suspected of being members of the resistance. Psychoundakis told Perkins it had happened the previous year when the Germans had made one of their rare incursions into the isolated region. They had combed the mountains for guerillas and shot most of the people they found. Several were innocent shepherds; other were villagers who had hidden through fear and not because of any real guilt.

Perkins, well shod with new boots, had no difficulty in keeping up with the leaders. Some of the Cretans had soled their boots with the tread of rubber tyres, giving a good foothold on the rocky trail. The pace was slow, in part because of the weight of the sovereigns. Before long Fielding admitted they were certainly heavy and he was gratified when Andonis Paterakis volunteered to relieve him. Andonis, a sturdy, lively adolescent with fine classic features, had earned a reputation as a tireless fighter with endurance beyond normal bounds.

As Perkins and his companions climbed higher, range after range of bare grey rock unfolded above terraced slopes. Groves of olive trees and small plots of potatoes punctured the pattern. A sweet-sour scent, all-pervading in the clear air, came from clumps of wild thyme, clinging tenaciously anywhere it could finger a root. High above in the golden light lay the Madara — the upper stone and shale reaches of the White Mountains, one of the island's three massive treeless formations.

The party trudged on. Exertion in the summer heat was tolerable only at a leisurely pace. When they reached the hideout the sun was beyond its zenith. Here Perkins found he was very much among friends. In the camp were several members of families who had given him food and shelter and practical aid when he was a straggler trying to escape from the island. He let his pack slip from his shoulders and slumped gratefully to the ground. Andonis had

103

carried the gold all the rest of the way and he, too, was glad to put down his load. The Cretans soon dropped off to sleep — it was siesta time anyway — and Perkins was not long in dozing too.

Pytharaki was an ideal campsite in a picturesque alpine setting. Cypresses fought pines for space on the steep slopes; cool, sweet water bubbled from a nearby mountain stream. The Germans seldom came near; for them to penetrate this wilderness they needed an expert guide, and no-one among the intensely patriotic communities below, in Koustoyérako and neighbouring villages, was likely to offer this service or be forced into doing so. The valleys and ravines that webbed the area severely hampered movement; anyone without local knowledge would soon become hopelessly lost.

A wireless station had been set up here more by chance than planning, prompted by the departure in May of the fifty-one stragglers rounded up by Tom Moir. In 1942, landings and evacuations had been carried out at places further east on the southern coast, convenient for the people manning the early wireless transmission and receiving station set up near Asi Gonia, in the Amari district, at the north-eastern end of the White Mountains. However increased German patrolling of the central south coast in later months made it very dangerous to continue using some of these landing sites. So for the evacuation of Tom Moir's party, collected together in the dell of Koukounara near Koystoyérako, a suitable nearby site was chosen. This was the desolate spot near the western end of the southern coast — Tripiti. Apart from Koustoyérako, the only villages in the vicinity were Livadas and Moni. The naval craft seconded to this task also landed stores and equipment, including a new wireless set intended as a standby for the Asi Gonia set which had been off the air for long periods, often because of difficulties in replacing or rectifying faulty components.

The transmitter was a weighty piece of equipment and it would have been a long and tiring haul to carry it over the rough mountain tracks for several days. Fielding decided to avoid the arduous trek by establishing this new station and camp. As the Germans were much less active in the south-west, life at the new site was more carefree with security providing few problems. The wireless operator, Alec Tarves, was able to do his job without fears of being disturbed by German patrols. His aerial could be left up and he had no need to stow his equipment in a safe hiding place after each transmission.

The occupants of the site had made themselves very comfortable. A hut of brushwood and tree branches housed equipment and stores and scented herbs. Shelters had been made with low stone walls, roofed with thick foliage supported by woven branches. Inside, the men slept on brushwood and herbal bedding. Betrayal by nearby villagers was unthinkable and the men wandered freely in broad daylight without qualms.

A constant problem was food. The spring water's health-giving properties had the effect of provoking appetite − not an advantage with food in short supply. Yet the men in the camp fared better than the villagers. Because of the Cretan code of hospitality, and because of their support for the resistance, the locals served the men food whenever they wandered among them. Often the guerrillas were invited down from the mountains to organised feasts. Several villagers had attached themselves to the camp and brought up sacks of beans, rice and large cheeses. But still the men were hungry.

A solution was found in the black market which flourished under encouragement from the Germans in the bomb-damaged, semi-derelict capital, Chanea. Regular supplies from the Chanea market began arriving in the camp to allevaite shortages in the camp larder. With Perkins' arrival at Pytharaki, bringing ample new supplies, the camp was no longer so dependent on local resources, and for the rest of the summer the agents and their helpers lived in comparative luxury. Cigarettes, were an important commodity in all supplies sent. Most of the *andartes* smoked and enjoyed the English brands; they were also needed to satisfy Fielding who was said to need ninety a day!

In the still air across the valley a cock heralded another day — the first of August. Dark sky beyond the alpine rock slowly flooded bright, its source hidden by the massive White Mountain range. Far below, fingers of white drifted lazily aloft. As burnished rays tickled the treetops, the camp began to stir; outpost sentries returned with nothing to report.

There was no reveille here as Perkins had known it, no stand to, no morning parade, no regimentation at all. He stretched sluggish limbs, stiff from the previous day's mountain hike. In the silence of awakening day every noise, every snapping branch, boot on stone, murmur of voice, was magnified to crystal clarity.

Perkins was alert and anxious to be assigned duties, to get into the action. But there was little for him immediately to do. Although he had come as Fielding's second-in-command, the situation had changed. Everything was now well organised; there were few problems with communications, and no longer was there need for Fielding to be away for long periods trudging through the more than two thousand square kilometres of his territory, holding conferences with guerrilla leaders.

Nor was there any real need for Perkins to be in command during Fielding's absences. The small band of guerrillas was capably led by thirty-year-old Vasili Paterakis, serene and imperturbable, whose sense of purpose and responsibility made him ideal for the task. It was felt unwise for a newcomer, not of their fraternity, to take command. With Vasili were his five younger brothers. Manolis Paterakis exuded an air of sophistication in spite of his peasant upbringing, while the highly strung Costis, in whom a crisis produced a calculated calmness, had the distinction of being a fine shot — a quality he was to display to great effect later on. Most handsome of the six was the burly Andonis, a daredevil whose strong features reminded one of Hollywood's Clark Gable. George, an introvert, proved reliable in emergency, while Vardis, the youngest, an adolescent with a fine singing voice, had not long since attained puberty. The six, together with several of their near relatives, formed a proficient fighting unit although serving mainly as guards and sentries.

George Psychoundakis had a lot to catch up on, especially the doings of twenty-four weeks since he had left for Cairo. Most of his day was taken up with animated chattering with fellow Cretans who were equally eager to know about George's experiences in the Middle East.

Psychoundakis had a comic sense of humour which endeared him to all the British agents. From the time the first stragglers reached his village of Asi Gonia, he had been helping the Allies, assisting the wounded and acting as a guide to places of safety and evacuation points. Nearly two years before, towards the end of 1941, the Psychoundakis family had been brought to near destitution. They lived in an area near the borders of the Sphakia region, renowned for its banditry and the fierceness of its inhabitants. Among their occupations the Sphakians included cattle rustling; apparently one night they had crossed into the Amari and stolen the family's flock of sixty sheep — the principal means of livelihood for the Psychoundakis parents and four children of whom George was the eldest, barely twenty at the beginning of the German occupation. For a family already poor, the theft spelt ruin.

With the arrival of the first British agents in that year, George was soon acting as a runner, carrying messages for Special Operations men established in widely separated places. Because he was dependable, possessed a keen intellect in spite of little schooling, and was eager and agile, the agents kept him rather busier than their other Cretan helpers. Small in stature though of manly age, he looked more like a boy, a notion encouraged by his ebullient

107

and clownish behaviour which had earned him the nickname of Bertodoulos (the Jester). When he became a runner for Patrick Leigh Fermor and Xan Fielding they coined for him the code-name of the Changeling, later altered to the Changebug. The cover name chosen for Perkins was Vasili, but among the British agents and Cretans with whom Perkins was most closely associated he was usually called Kiwi to distinguish him from the eldest of the Paterakis brothers.

Fielding (code-name Aleko) suggested to Perkins that he should first become acquainted with the people in the organisation, going out to meet them with George Psychoundakis as his guide. At the same time George could be reunited with his family in Asi Gonia. Fielding gave Perkins a letter to deliver to one of the movement's most staunch supporters, George Alevizakis, who lived in the village of Argyroupolis, further down in the valley below Asi Gonia. Perkins was delighted to be on the move and, having come to know Psychoundakis well on the journey from Cairo, was pleased George had been chosen to escort him.

Next day, night had scarcely succumbed to the first flush of dawn when Perkins shouldered a *sakouli* and followed Psychoundakis out of the camp. With them went two others — George Phindrikalis, returning to the same home village as Psychoundakis, and Stelio Vernadakis. Those who saw them leave watched as they disappeared into the forest of pine and cypress; a green patchwork across the mountainside.

In the cool morning air the going was easy though the slopes were steep. In the full light of day some two hours later, they reached eagle-height and the place known as Achlada. Here, rugged peaks standing sentinel over its seclusion, the villagers of Koustoyérako had their summer *mytata* — the huts comprising the sheepfold where they made their cheese from the milk of sheep and goats. Established in the 1930's. From thyme fires came a pungent aroma as shepherds cooked breakfast and passed round a common yoghurt pot. It was a place Dudley Perkins was later to have cause to remember.

Out on the open mountainside, above the forest, the trail led over rough stones, flanked by rockslides, scrawny scrub and yawning chasms. If one searches assiduously among the stunted brushwood it is possible to find the rare Cretan herb, Origanum *dyctamnus,* whose healing powers have been admired since Homer's time, and from which a few hardy mountaineers make a tenous living. The bushes, with unpretentious purple blossoms, tend to prefer precipitous rock faces and people risk their lives to gather it because the aromatic essence is much prized for used in perfumes and for flavouring liqueurs. Its popular name (Erontas) arises from its reputation as a potent aphrodisiac.

The group took the steep slopes at a comfortable angle, sweating under a scorching sun bouncing its heat off the harsh granite. Above, the naked rock of the Lefka Ori was as dazzling white as its winter caps, some twenty of its peaks towering over 1800 metres. On the top of one of these, Gingilos, they rested at about 2000 metres. Spread below to the north was a lush flat carpet, the great upland plain of the Omalos, summer garden of Chanea, leading into the great gorge of Samaria, overhung by the grey cliffs of Gingilos.

Psychoundakis told Perkins he might well see the local inhabitants — the *agrimia,* the distinctive Cretan Ibexes. These wild mountain goats — now strictly protected by law — have roamed the island for thousands of years; they are found today only in this region and on an offshore island. Adornments picked up in the ruins of the Minoan city of Knossos, near Heraklion, depict their characteristic curved horns and slim bodies. *Agrimia* meat was considered the best obtainable and a real luxury during the Occupation.

But of greater moment was to be on the watch for the enemy. The Omalos presented a hazard for Perkins' party — the Germans had a guard post here. Patrols were sent out to observe the movements of unwary resistance fighters and to lie in ambush on the trails. Yet all below looked peaceful, the wild beauty of the Omalos, surrounded by bare and jagged limestone, glorious to behold. Stone huts around the edge of the plain were the seasonal refuges of shepherds from the lowland villages. The land held crops of wheat, potatoes and beans, providing cover for partridges and hares. Olives and mulberries were swelling ahead of harvest. On the light breeze drifted the music of sheepbells. In three months the shepherds would have retreated to the lowlands and by the New Year the plain would be snowbound. In those troubled times the industrious growers could not expect to reap the reward of their labours: the Nazi occupiers would seize the best of the crops, and what was not lost that way might well be stolen by hungry raiders.

Since it would be rash to try to cross the Omalos, Psychoundakis led the party downhill to the south of the plain towards the gorge. Extreme caution was observed, reconnaissance made of every section of the precipitous way — the Germans had lately given the route special attention. Progress was consequently slow.

The sheepfolds belonging to the Viglis family came in sight and they saw several figures moving about nearby. Prudence dictated concealment. Use of binoculars from their hiding place confirmed their fears: the men were Germans.

Perkins wanted George to flank them, but Psychoundakis said there was no other way. They had no option but to stay hidden and wait. It was a long, hot, frustating day and the Germans did not budge. They were evidently from the post on the Omalos as late in the afternoon they left, travelling in the direction of the plain.

At the sheepfold only members of the Viglis family remained, and when it was safe to leave their cover the four moved down to be welcomed with hearty embraces. They gratefully received yoghurt offered as refreshment, but resisted an invitation to stay: the

Germans·had held them up too long and the need was to move on. The shepherds consequently produced fresh cheese for the four to take with them.

Shadows slid up the mountainside as the heat swept out of the day, and the diminishing light brought with it a sharp chill. Psychoundakis had hoped to be further ahead and on the lower slopes by dusk, but when they could no longer see their way, they had to make the best of it overnight at the higher altitude.

Above loomed a peak of striking symbolism for the young Psychoundakis, fired by the inspiration of a man whose very name stood for what Cretans were fighting for − freedom. While Mount Venizelos awakened warmth in the hearts of the three Cretans, its chilly cloak gave the travellers a bitter night in their unprotected bivouac. Unable to sleep, they were up with the first flush in the east, slapping and chafing numbed limbs. As they shouldered their *sakoulis* Psychoundakis glanced up at the peak, but he saw no eagle sitting upon this high mountain as in Elevtherios Venizelos' symbolic poem which he is said to have written squatting atop it and planning the revolution which eventually brought Crete's union with Greece. Later Premier of Greece and founder of Greece's Liberal Party, Venizelos is regarded as the father of the modern Greek nation.

The going, now all downhill, was easier as they headed northeast and reached the vegetation of the northern foothills. By this time Perkins was beginning to feel that he had regained the mountain feet of the hard apprenticeship of his year as a straggler.

Soon there were wild flowers in profusion, the red flame of oleanders, hedgerows of grey-green agaves, grotesquely shaped cacti; and then small orchards, vineyards, cultivated patches and olive groves. As on the previous day Perkins and his companions were thwarted by the presence of Germans. They had tramped most of the day and were in sight of the tiny village of Tsakistra when they spied enemy soldiers a short distance away, their backs

111

towards the travellers. They quickly turned and sought cover. For a time they kept the Germans under observation, hoping they would move. It had been intended to stay in Tsakistra that night, but this now seemed impossible since the Germans showed no sign of departing. Their way thus barred, Perkins and his companions set off for Kyriakosselia, to the east.

Here, Psychoundakis led them to the home of Levtheri Koura-kis, whose family were staunch helpers of the resistance. Levtheri told them that German patrols were particularly active at that time and it would be dangerous to stay in his house. He guided them to secluded rocky shelters outside the village where the group was much less likely to be discovered.

Next day Psychoundakis was awake early, excited at the prospect of reaching his village of Asi Gonia and being reunited with his family whom he had not seen for six months. He kept to upland trails, skirting the villages of Pemonia and Phre. Near midday he was unable to resist the temptation to move lower towards the main road, well used by German patrols and convoys, in order to introduce Perkins to the Vandoulakis family whom he knew would give them food. Their households of men and women, young and old, all possessed the warlike qualities of their ancestors; since the Occupation they had been loyally steadfast in giving shelter to British agents and resistance fighters. Xan Fielding in particular had been well looked after by them during his period in this part of Crete the previous year.

To Psychoundakis and others, Nicholas Vandoulakis was affectionately known as 'Uncle' Niko. In his vineyard, near the large village of Nippoi, the party rested. The grapes were ripe and swollen and they feasted on these, along with food brought to them from the village by family members.

The home of Uncle Niko — in nearby Vaphe — was a real oasis. Right from the start of the Occupation he had fed and sheltered many of the New Zealand, Australian and British stragglers who passed that way — to the extent that the house became known among locals as the 'British Consulate'.

With appetites well satisfied, Perkins, Psychoundakis and Phindrilakis climbed again for the last stage to Asi Gonia, while Stelio Vernadakis, bound for Vryses, went his own way. The garden landscape vanished where the mountains rose. By evening, the trio were high above a cluster of white stone and mud houses. Though tempted to move down to the family home, Psychoundakis felt that a rash action on his part could put all of them in danger. In the lee of one of the high peaks known as Drapona the three spent the night in the open in safety.

Next day, Perkins and Psychoundakis moved down to a cheesehut owned by George's cousin Marko. George Phindrilakis went on alone, negotiating the rocks and boulders on the upper reaches of the pass in which Asi Gonia stands. From below, as from above, there was no road; it could only be reached on foot. He would see his own family and learn if there was any danger.

It was just a week since Perkins had landed back in Crete. So far it had been fairly tame, lacking the kind of dangers he had experienced when he had been trying to escape from the island. Caution, and the good sense of his guide, had prevented encounters with the enemy which they would have had difficulty coming through unscathed. All day they waited. Phindrilakis had not returned to warn them off, and there was no untoward activity in the village. Psychoundakis assessed that it would be safe to enter, and at nightfall they scrambled down over the stones.

George led Perkins down narrow stony lanes of small, rough, whitewashed houses, the ground dotted with cactuses and plane trees, past springs where the villagers drew their water, until at the bottom of the villge they reached his home. When Psychoundakis entered there were shrieks of delight and surprise. His father and mother embraced him in tight bearhugs, with much slapping of arms, kissing of cheeks and words of affection. Cretan welcomes are nothing if not demonstrative. Usually news of a pending arrival will precede a traveller, so efficient is the Cretan grapevine, but the Psychoundakis household had had no forewarning.

Perkins was introduced to George's father, an old man crumpled by adversity but still proud; his mother, Angelike, was small, skinny, and with smiling, sparkling eyes. George's two sisters and brother were all younger — Rodianthe, fifteen, Eleni, thirteen, and brother Nicolas yet to reach adolescence. As Perkins observed, it was the kind of poverty — in western terms — he had already seen in many another mountain village, but it was a home, and he was cordially welcomed. In the single, almost bare room, its floor trampled earth, was a dilapidated table, a couple of old chairs, a mule saddle, an ikon or two. Wooden struts supported an earthen roof. Cooking was done in an open hearth in the manner of ancient times, the smoke escaping through a makeshift chimney. Along one wall ran a raised ledge on which the family slept with whatever rough coverings they possessed.

It was good to be in a warm room for a change, to eat and drink indoors. Excitedly the family brought out wine and *raki* and delved into their small food store for cheese and olives. For hours they talked until long past time for bed. The family wanted them to stay the rest of the night but George had no wish to endanger his kin so refused to take the risk that he and Perkins might be caught in a dawn search. Outside the village the men found a sheltered place to sleep.

On the following day a message was sent to Argyroupolis for George Alevizakis to come to meet Perkins in Asi Gonia. As well as the letter Perkins carried he also had money for Alevizakis, who was able to give good value for the payments he received. Most of it went on food and clothing for the British agents and their Cretan helpers. Other expenses included bribes to German officials and people in their employ, and maintenance of a special squad of armed men organised to mete out punishment to traitors and col-

114

laborators. Usually this meant death: more than one 'bad Greek' was shot by the squad in his own house.

After another day in Asi Gonia, Perkins set off to return to Selino in the company of George Phindrilakis. George Psychoundakis, after so long away in the Middle East, wanted to stay longer with his family and learn more of what had been going on in his absence. He heard about the efforts of the Germans to find Xan Fielding's hideout and the wireless set in the stony terrain above Asi Gonia, of the retribution meted out to the traitors who aided the Germans in their search, how the villagers of Asi Gonia had remained loyal and protected Fielding and his helpers, hiding them, feeding them, shifting their stores, explosives and the wireless set while the Germans searched fruitlessly. It was this harassment which led Fielding to go to Selino for temporary refuge and later to decide on the new station above Koustoyérako.

During the return journey Phindrilakis took Perkins to meet the fighting detachment of Petros Petrakis in the mountains above Asi Gonia, and in the Askifou area he got to know the guerrillas led by another resistance leader, Manoussos Karkarnis. Some time later he met the resistance groups organised by the well-known and very active Vandoulas family and familiarised himself with the Apokoronas area and the conditions there. By the third week of August, Psychoundakis had rejoined the camp in Selino.

Round the high mountains, round the peaks swirls the air,
But earth and heroism are not found every day.

— Cretan *rizitika*

EIGHT
Marking Time

Even with so many trials, still life is sweet,
And anyone who wants Charos to come, he must be mad.

— Cretan *rizitika*

In the guerillas' mountain camp above Koustoyérako, life for Perkins during the rest of August and September was nothing if not
easygoing. He was enjoying the fresh mountain air and outdoor
life, which reminded him of his days as a youth, camping in Otago
and in the foothills of the Southern Alps. Day after day a scorching
sun burned through a limpid sapphire sky. Stripped half naked,
Perkins acquired a gold-brown tint as he went cheerfully about his
chores. He enjoyed the feeling of well-being, and the comparative
inactivity did not bother him.

Vasili Paterakis was well in control of his small band of brothers
and relatives and Perkins' main function when Fielding was away
was to provide companionship for Alec Tarves. Apart from being
conscientious and professionally efficient, Tarves added a pleasant
liveliness to the camp. Cheerful obscenities and mighty oaths
flowed unceasingly from him, uttered so good-humouredly and
without rancour that it was impossible to take offence.

The New Zealander's penchant for improvisation allowed him to
find a use for discarded biscuit tins from the stores: he constructed
an oven — the only one in any of the mountain camps. This allowed him to apply knowledge of the culinary art, turning the
large stocks of foodstuffs which came with him from Cairo into tas-

116

ty meals.

German patrols in the area were still scarce and it was possible to move around fairly freely. Village people often visited the hideout and brought raki, wine and food — *khorta* (spinach) soaked in oil, occasionally an egg or two, beans and potatoes. Whenever men in the camp went down the mountain into the villages, people always insisted in giving hospitality in spite of their own very real shortages. Sometimes these village visits would spontaneously turn into feasts and almost miraculously sheepmeat and other ingredients for a spree would appear.

But this situation was soon to change. The Germans began sending more patrols up the mountains and into the high villages. Fielding discovered this when he set out on a tour of places he had not yet visited in order to learn the people's views on a developing political situation which, on mainland Greece, had led to rival resistance factions attacking one another.

There was a danger of the same thing happening in Crete. British agents, with full authority, had officially recognised E.O.K. (the National Organisation of Crete) as the island's chief and most influential resistance group rather than the growing Communistled E.A.M. (National Liberation Front — the political organisation) and its allied military arm, E.L.A.S., the Greek Popular Liberation Army. Unfortunately, the British Military Headquarters in the Middle East, with great reluctance, had been pressured into recognising E.A.M./E.L.A.S. on the mainland as a means of gaining Greek co-operation for S.O.E.'s. sabotage raids there. In this, as subsequent events proved, their agents in the field were badly let down.

In Crete, the E.A.M./E.L.A.S. leader, General Emmanouel Mandakas, was a regular officer, a Cretan — a burly man, slow of movement, laboured in speech, with a tendency to be pompous yet displaying a commanding presence. Mainland recognition led him to insist upon the same authority to be accorded to his own groups. But the situation in Crete was different. From his own perceptions Fielding knew that the majority of Cretan villagers were loyal to E.O.K. in spite of Communist attempts to disparage the National Organisation. The matter became of some concern because General Mandakas had moved his headquarters to the Selino area in order to take advantage of the comparative absence of German activity in the region, and he was trying to corrupt the Allies' own sympathisers with Communist propaganda. Mandakas was also demanding arms for his men from the Allies. Fielding considered, in the light of these developments, that it would be expedient to travel more widely through his neighbourhood and the area he commanded to counter the Communist propaganda as well as feeling the pulse of village opinion.

On his first day out the British agent was fortunate to escape capture — or worse. He took with him three men from the camp, including Vasili Paterakis. Before they had got very far they ran unexpectedly into a German patrol at close quarters. Bullets flew all around them as they tried to escape. Fielding and one of his companions hid in undergrowth; the other pair disappeared elsewhere. Suddenly a piercing cry came from one of the Germans, wounded either by crossfire from his comrades or by one of the Cretans, and the firing stopped. After attending to their wounded member the Germans organised a thorough search for Fielding and his companion, spraying the bushes with bullets and hurling hand grenades. Miraculously, the pair were not hit as they hugged the ground in the thick shrubbery. At times in their search, the Germans were only a couple of metres away. They enlisted the help of people from a nearby village, expecting to find two bodies, and the hunt went on all day until sunset. Not knowing if any of the searchers were still near, Fielding took no chances. He and his companion did not leave their hiding place until after midnight, and only then did they steal away with extreme caution.

Because of the danger from this greater interest in the Koustoyérako area by the Germans, Fielding felt it prudent to strengthen his defences in this hitherto fairly secure region. More men were eager to join the small numbers already in the Pytharaki camp and they needed only food and arms to ensure their formation into a reasonable combat group. Fielding asked Cairo by wireless for supplies to be dropped. For the first attempt, Perkins, Fielding and a group of Cretans which included George Psychoundakis climbed from their lair through the forest to the high open ground at Achlada. They collected brushwood for the signal fires, and waited. From the darkness to the south they heard the unmistakable drone of an aircraft and lit the fires. The plane passed overhead and a few of the parachutes and their containers were found. After searching all through the night they had acquired only a few pistols, some money and a wireless set, much to their disappointment.

As daylight filtered through the mountain mist the group prepared to descend to the hideout. But the morning revealed an amazing sight. Below, on treetops on the steep slopes, lay brilliant white patches. Soon, with great glee, clutching hands in high branches were unfastening loaded containers from parachute cords and dropping them earthwards. Parachutes, too, were hauled down. To leave them would advertise the airdrop to the Germans, who probably knew there had been one anyway; the material would be useful in some way as well. It took most of the day to collect the packages and carry the contents down the mountainside to the camp. A second drop was later made with greater accuracy, some parachutes landing almost on the signal fires.

Several men had been making do with worn clothing and battered boots; to them the new supplies were a real morale booster. Strong boots were essential; rough mountain trekking soon battered leather footwear. Though it seems macabre, bodies of men who had been executed would often be dug up afterwards at night merely to get their boots. And anyone leaving the island for Egypt was always expected to leave his boots for a needy person staying behind. Rubber tyres which were cut up to resole worn boots were often stolen from German lorries left unguarded; occasionally a German vehicle would be ambushed to strip it of its tyres.

The clothing from the two airdrops included uniforms and Australian-style hats. An assortment of easily handled machine-guns, ammunition, grenades and subversive leaflets were also supplied. In the days that followed, the *andartes* at Pytharaki and other resistance fighters in the Selino area were outfitted from the new stock and given weapons and ammunition. Some of the money was sent to Infantry Colonel Christos Tsiphakis – a regular Greek officer leading the resistance in Prine who was also Rethymnon area head of E.O.K. – and more was distributed to several of the Allies' staunchest helpers. Many of them gave help and food without any thought of reward, but in such hard times this tangible form of recognition was returned a hundredfold.

The extent of loyalty for E.O.K. made the work of Allied agents in Crete far easier than on mainland Greece. In Western Crete, particularly, support for E.A.M./E.L.A.S. was successfully countered by British agents with the help of respected Cretan officials. Eleftherios Venizelos' legacy of liberal republican tradition was embedded in his native Crete; E.O.K., predominantly republican, was sufficiently broadminded to have a catholic membership. As Colonel Montague Woodhouse says in his study of Greek wartime and post-war politics, *Apple of Discord,* the internal freemasonry of Cretan blood is so strong that even a Cretan royalist can be trusted and forgiven because he is a Cretan. One of E.O.K.'s political leaders, Emmanuel Papadhoyiannis, was a royalist who was greatly respected, but the organisation drew the line at allowing in anyone with Communist leanings. This bond of blood enabled agents in Crete to produce a great measure of unity with harmony in the common cause.

Just before Perkins' arrival back on the island the Cretans had been misled by a broadcast made by the King of Greece, George II, who with Crown Prince Paul had left Greek soil from Crete four days after the start of the battle for the island – in company, incidentally, with New Zealand soldiers acting as guards. In the broadcast the King called upon all Greeks to co-operate with Allied servicemen landing on their shores. Cretans, along with Greek mainlanders, interpreted this wrongly as meaning that they were about to be liberated. That sparked a disastrous crusade by Kapetan Manoli Bandouvas in Eastern Crete – when an Allied invasion failed to materialise Cretans felt betrayed.

What the broadcast was intended to convey was only that they should help the raiding parties that were being sent in. The message, in fact, was part of a bluff over Allied plans – giving the Germans the impression that the next thrust would be against Greece, thereby diverting attention from the imminent invasion of Sicily.

While the Occupation lasted, E.O.K. dominated political and resistance activity. The Greek Communist Party (K.K.E.) and the Communist-controlled E.A.M./E.L.A.S. failed to gain any significant following. Denied British support, Mandakas and his men received little encouragement from the population; dissappointed over his failure, Mandakas left Crete later in 1943 to join E.L.A.S.'s General Headquarters in mainland Greece, becoming for a time Chief of Staff. In 1944, on 25 March, Greece's Independence Day, Mandakas was appointed Minister of War in the Political Committee of Greek Resistance (P.E.E.A.) which claimed to be a government of the liberated Greek people in the mountains. P.E.E.A. represented itself as a provisional government, independent of any émigré Greek set-up and professed loyalty to the Allied cause though firmly Communist-controlled. This lasted only a few weeks.

Manoli Bandouvas was one of E.O.K.'s chief leaders in the field, along with Georgios Petrakoyiorgis – both perpetuating the traditions of the Kapetanios heritage. Petrakoyiorgis, tall and bearded,

121

among the first to take to the mountains to establish himself as a guerilla leader, was a wealthy merchant with much influence before the war. He provided the money needed for arms and food to maintain his band, giving him a head start over others seeking to be chiefs of Pallikaria. Nonetheless when the british began financing resistance and sabotage in Crete, Petrakoyiorgis received his due share. Genuine patriotism inspired E.O.K. and assured its unity until the liberation in May 1945 after four years of deprivation, hunger, Nazi barbarism and committed struggle. In the first elections after the war, Crete voted against King George II who had returned to Greece. He died in March 1947, his brother Paul then succeeding to the throne — a man less controversial and acceptable to the Cretans.

With constant contact with Cretans in the camp and with local villagers, Perkins increased his command of Greek with its dialectal Cretan accent and idiom. One day he returned to the Pytharaki hideout after a day's hunting with a bag of hares.

'He was holding a German gun and nine hares,' Vasili Paterakis remembers. 'Aleko (Fielding) embraced him and later we cleaned them before cooking. Aleko said: "Separate the lean flesh from the bones, and throw the bones away."

'Well, we cleaned them and separated the meat, but Costis cut up the bones to cook them. Aleko laughed at this. And when they were cooked Costis offered some to Aleko, saying: "You should have some bones too!" '

Another story relates to prediction and foreboding. There was a time when the camp was well supplied with about forty lambs and the men killed two to provide a meal. As they were being cooked in a boiler, one of the Paterakis uncles was removing the flesh. He held up a shoulder-blade (associated in ancient belief with a capability to foretell future events) and said: 'By noon tomorrow someone from this post will no longer be with us.'

Next days, says Vasili Paterakis, his uncle told him that one of the fighters from the camp had been killed by the Germans.

'After that, Vasili (Perkins) of blessed memory, used to say when an attack was being planned on the Germans in the mountains: "Fetch the Cretan radio (the shoulder blade of the lamb)!" '

As well as being cook, Perkins took on the role of nurse when occasion demanded. One of the bravest, most trustworthy and hard-working of the runners and guides, Yanni Vandoulas, from the village of Nippos, has reason to be thankful for Perkins' nursing after an incident in the mountains. After six days away delivering money to Colonel Tsiphakis, Psychoundakis returned early in the morning of 19 September without Yanni who had been his companion on the mission, and aroused the slumbering camp in an attempt to get someone to go out and search for his comrade. Perkins heard how the pair had run into outlaws who lived by thieving and stealing sheep − 'wind boys' the Cretans called them − while coming back through Samaria Gorge. The two runners had chosen this route when a shepherd had warned them to avoid a large German patrol which was moving towards the Omalos, their intended way.

When the outlaws had called upon them from a distance to stop, Yanni had run off. The outlaws had begun firing and shouted that the pair would be killed if they did not stay where they were. George hid, but Yanni continued running. When the outlaws came up and began searching, George bravely came out of hiding and talked his way out of what could have become a nasty confrontation.

Psychoundakis continued on his way, travelling by moonlight through the night, and reached the camp still in darkness. He then poured out his tale to sleepy-eyed men but no-one was willing to go out then to look for Yanni. Later, at daybreak, one of the men went to the spring for water. He returned with Yanni, blood-stained from a wound. A bullet had passed right through his forearm. Yanni explained that it had happened during the firing; he had run on and hidden until he thought it was safe to come out. Then he had made his way back, arriving a little after George.

Perkins took charge of the wounded man, cleaned the wound and dressed it with medical supplies from the recent drop. Meanwhile, someone was sent to a hideout of Cretan patriots nearby where there was known to be a Selino surgeon, Doctor Pentaris. At first the doctor thought he would have to amputate Yanni's hand, but he deferred his decision, telling Perkins to release the bandage on the arm every hour to let blood flow until next time he called. The wound looked much better when the doctor returned, and although Yanni kept his hand, he was able to use only one or two of his fingers after it had completely healed.

On another occasion, several weeks later, Perkins is credited with saving the life of one of his young fighters through careful nursing. The Cretan boy, shot through the chest, was in a bad way. He was taken to a Cretan doctor who told Perkins that the wound was a severe one and he could not save him. But Perkins refused to accept this verdict. Encouraging the boy not to give up the fight, he tended him through a critical stage. Then, with the young lad in a stable condition, Perkins arranged for his evacuation to Egypt for further treatment and recovery.

NINE

The Bandouvas Factor

Opposite me stands Erotas and he displays his armour
Which he throws at me, both the fire and the splendour.

— Cretan *mantinade*

Towards the end of September a runner arrived in camp with a
message for Fielding from Tom Dunbabin, who was in command
in Eastern Crete. Tom wanted to meet Xan in the centre of the
island, near Asi Gonia, but gave no reason. Fielding asked Perkins
to accompany him, and they took with them three of the "boys':
Psychoundakis, Pavlo Vernadakis - both of whom had had spells
of ttraining in Egypt - and Manoli Gyparis.

At the Viglis family's sheepfold at the Poria they met Roussos
Viglis - who had warned Psychoundakis and Yanni Vandoulas of
the presence of Germans when they had passed that way a few
days previously. Roussos told the group that the man who had
shot Yanni was his nephew; the youth had shamed him and he
wished him dead. When the party reached the Apokoronas region
at the north-eastern fringe of the White Mountains it divided.
Perkins went with Psychoundakis and Manoli to Asi Gonia, taking
with them Greek money (about a million drachmas) to be left with
Manoli's uncle, Pavlo Gyparis, one of the British agent's staunchest
henchmen. As usual, it was for buyinh food for the resistance
fighters and for service members passing that way.

Later Perkins continued with Manoli to Alones, an isolated

village on the route south to Rhodakino and chosen as the site for the next boat arrival on the south coast. There, a second attempt was to be made to evacuate the powerful guerrilla leader. Kapetan Manoli Bandouvas. Bandouvas, expecting that an Allied landing was imminent, had ambushed German convoys and inflicted severe casualties. As a result the Commanding General in Crete, General Miller (nicknamed "the Butcher") had ordered a pinitive operation in the Vianos district; villages were burned and hundreds of innocent civilians massacred in the search for the guerrilla leader whose stock with Cretans dropped markedly because of his foolishness. With his small force dispersed and on the run, he had to ask theBritish to take him off the island.

On this first occasion, however, the boat had had to leave without them because of worsening seas after half the passengers had been embarked. Those who did get away were Italians; after Italy's surrender. Captain Paddy Leigh Fermor had gone to Eastern Crete, occupied by an Itlian division under General Carta, in order to disarm the garrison. During negotiations in the Lasithi capital, Neapolis, Leigh Fermor had persuaded General Carta and some of his staff to withdraw to Egypt. For the evacuation, the British agent had led them across the mointains to the south coast, dodging German units entering the region to take over the Italians' duties. After the Italian general and his party boarded the boat, Lieutenant Bob Young decided that the deteriorating weather would not allow the embarkation to continue and Bandouvas' group of forty was left on the shore. Leigh Fermor, who had escorted the general aboard, was unable to return to land and unexpectedly ended up to Egypt.

Arriving on that occasion - on a mid-southern beach close to Tris Ekklisies - was Sandy Rendel, who had been Perkins' conducting officer some weeks earlier. Rendel recalls seeing General Carta going out to the motor launch as he was being ferried in. In the rough water some of the stores being landed were lost overboard.

126

And on shore was Bandouvas, fuming when he realised that Bob Young was leaving without waiting for him.

Bandouvas, a village chieftain and the eldest of five brothers, was dressed in the typical garb of the pallikari. Dark complexioned, brawny and sporting a large black bristly moustache, he spoke with a deep, husky voice and was given to ostentatious shows of authority.

There were heated discussions between Tom Dunbabin and Bandouvas, who felt he had been betrayed by the British. The situation may have become nasty: in his annoyance Bandouvas could well have ordered his guerrilla band to wipe out the British agents. The S.O.E. men were on their guard while Dunbabin gave Bandouvas an assurance that he would get him and his party off on the next boat.

The British agents and the guerrillas retired into the hills to consider the situation. Having been thwarted in his bid to leave the island, Bandouvas now appeared to be wavering, but after prolonged discussions with his men and with the agents he agreed to leave on a boat due to arrive at Rhodakino, further west. The British hope was that his departure would leave the Germans no need to continue operations to capture him - marauding, burning, pillaging and killing innocent people in the process.

Rendel moved east to his assignment in Lasithi, while Dunbabin and Bandouvas made their way in the opposite direction to a meeting with Fielding.

For the planned new evacuation, the chosen assembly point was a col called Tsilivdika, above Alones. From this high place the departure beach lay directly to the south. As word was discreetly put out about the rendezvous, the exposed slopes of Tsilivdika became, in a matter of a day and a half, a huge camp of armed bravadoes. Bandouvas and several of his henchmen were there with Dunbabin, Fielding and men of the intelligence gathering organisation, the Inter-Services Liaison Department, including

Captain John Stanley and Captain Ralph Stockbridge; they were joined by resistance men from surrounding villages - Photeinou, Alones, Vilandredo and Rhodakino.

Food brought to the gathering of about eighty was soon consumed. A sheep was roasted over an open fire and more food was prepared in a large iron container set over flaming wood. During the evening of 3 October a shepherd named Manolis Ergazakis, who was alleged to be a traitor, was brought in. Around the fire all night, under a sky full of stars, an impromptu court martial was conducted by the Cretans, the prisoner sitting on bare stones, his hands tied behind his back.

Bandouvas said he had been looking for Ergazakis for some time since he left the village of Katelli Pediada in the area Bandouvas had controlled. The man well knew the kind of punishment he could expect. A short time before, Bandouvas' men had dealt with another traitor. The man had been hung upside down while the guerrillas casually stuck knives into him. His screams had attracted one of the British agents, and the guerrillas desisted only when they were told that acting in this way they were no better than their German oppressors.

It was nearly dawn before the interrogation and the depositions were brought to an end. Ergazakis confessed he had been recruited by the quisling police chief in Heraklion, a Cretan named Polioudakis, to spy on his countrymen and on the British. Relatives of some of the guerrillas were among those he was thought to have betrayed. In pleading for mercy the man named others who had been similarly recruited as agents of the Germans. He claimed he had left his old district to escape working for the Gestapo and he asked Bandouvas to pardon him. But it was believed that Ergazakis might well still be in German employ. No decision about his fate had been made when Bandouvas declared it was time for sleep, and the prisoner was put under guard.

At daybreak on 4 October, sentries spied a party of Germans

and Italians moving up the mountain and roused the camp. At the same time a group of resistance men from Asi Gonia, led by Pavlo Gyparis, was approaching. One of the founders of the Cretan resistance movement, Kapetan Petro Petrakis, was with them, and the arrival of this experienced band of fighters, already successful in tussling with the enemy, added considerable strength to the gathering now engaged in defence. The newcomers scuttled into safety as the guerrillas began firing.

Given to acting precipitately, the Cretans had begun shooting before Perkins or other British agents could instruct them to hold off until the patrol was much closer and consequently only one of the enemy, an Italian, was killed. Another Italian surrendered, but all the Germans took off at speed and escaped. The incident sealed the fate of the traitor - at uch a time of danger a man whose loyalty was suspect was a liability. A single shot was fired into his head before the guerrillas gave chase in small groups.

For the next hour there were sounds of fighting over a wide area, giving the impression that a battle was in progress. The pursuers ferrreted out and killed all the enemy force, except for one badly wounded Italian. He was questioned and then Niko Souris - a Greek who had worked before the war in Alexandria, and who had joined the S.O.E. - was detailed to end the Italians's sufferings, Niko subsequently admitted he was too soft-hearted to kill in cold blood, and the man was left to die in his own time.

Shortly afterwards, the guerrillas learned that another enemy force was bearing down on them. They quickly deployed and took cover. Holding fire this time until the enemy was within range, they killed all except the leader, who escaped, and a Greek in German uniform, acting as a guide. The Greek, surprised by two of the guerrillas, had immediately shouted in his own language that he was surrendering and not to shoot. His German rifle was taken away and, on questioning, he claimed he had been forced into helping the Germans because of his knowledge of their

129

language: he was merely an interpreter, working for his food. This information left the guerrillas uncertain as to what they should do with him.

The escaped German leader then made the mistake of revealing himself to fire on Psychoundakis and a comrade who had set off to take a woman and her children to safety in a nearby village. Alerted by the shooting, one of the guerrillas took aim at the running German and felled him. Among papers found on the body was a message giving details of the gathering at Tsilivdika; this was shown to the captured Greek who denied all knowledge of the note and of the man who had signed and sent it. The guerrillas were not satisfied and devised another method to establish the facts.

With the guerrillas, under the protection of wireless operator Captain Ralph Stockbridge (code-name Michalaki, later Siphi), was a German deserter named August. In a pantomime procedure, indicating that both were to be executed, August was placed under guard with the Greek prisoner. Soon the two were talking softly. August said he was a German officer and berated his countrymen for not sending a force in the wake of so much shooting so that they could be rescued. The Greek then revealed his true colours. He told the German not to worry since a battalion should be moving up. The small patrol he had been with had been sent ahead to verify the accuracy of the information in the note. The Greek added he had been working with the Germans ever since their arrival. August was then withdrawn and he repeated to the British agents what the Greek had told him. The Greek, questioned again, persisted he was only an interpreter. Bandouvas ordered him killed at once and, led by two guerrillas to a nearby cave, the traitor was shot twice in the head. The German deserter, whose life the British were preserving against the guerrillas' will, was due to be sent to Egypt on the next boat.

With the knowledge that a large enemy force was likely shortly to appear, Perkins and the other agents helped contrive a plan of defence. The alternative to standing and fighting was abandonment of the evacuation and dispersal of the guerrillas. Bandouvas decided that with the departure set for that night, the risk of being able to fight off an attack was worth taking. First, the guerrillas collected all the German and Italian dead and threw them into chasms or into holes in the ground. Then they moved up to the top of the mountain range and took cover behind rocks and boulders. When the Germans arrived they were thus unable to identify the battle scene and the defenders, not being harassed, had no need to reveal their positions. It was later learned that the enemy troops, failing to find the guerrillas, had terrorised the local population is an attempt to extract information about the exact whereabouts of the gathering.

Papers taken from the bodies of German dead before their disposal made interesting reading. Nearly everyone in the group was on lists of those whom the Feldgendarmerie wanted to capture. The British agents were named with all their local pseudonyms and aliases, their physical descriptions and the activities in which they had taken part. Most of the details seemed fairly accurate and pointed to a good deal of assiduous intelligence, some probably from resistance men tortured for information before execution, some no doubt from 'bad Greeks' working for the Germans.

In the evening, the agents and the guerrillas moved down to the evacuation beach at Rhodakino. For several hours they waited and signalled. When the boat failed to appear it was decided to move up the mountains while it was still dark to find concealment for the day. On the way they passed through the ruins of the hillside village of Rhodakino - its ghostly remains charred, a sickly smell of burned flesh mingling with whiffs of smoke from still-smouldering embers. It was the village nearest to where a German had been killed in the countryside and was consequently chosen for reprisal.

131

Most Rhodakiniots, expecting retaliation, had fled; those who remained were given no mercy. They were shot, and their bodies burned along with their houses.

Bearing westwards as they climbed; Perkins, the other agents and the guerrillas reached the Skaloti gorge. There they rested. They were joined by refugees who reported that the village of Alones had been subjected to the Germans' attentions, but they had no news of the extent of the destruction or killings.

The Germans were now out in strength all through this mountainous area and it was becoming diificult to keep together such a large group - now nearly a hundred - without being discovered. Good fieldcraft enabled them to make progress north-westwards while dodging the searchers. They clambered over steep slopes and slithered down ravines for hour after hour. When eventually they found a reasonable spot to spend the night - at a place known as Manika - few slept because of the need to remain alert and not be surprised by a German patrol. By now, too, their bodies were sore from lying on rock surfaces.

As the ground mist began lifting into the brigteneing day the resistance group was shaken from drowsiness by the rattle of machine-gun fire about a kilometre away. It was in the village of Kallikrati; soon smoke began rising from the houses. Perkins and his companions decided to steal further away from this new danger.

. Two shepherds who later brought them cheese gave details of what happened. During the night the Germans had surrounded the village - their classic raiding method - and in the morning had entered, flushing the villagers from their homes. The Germans demanded that any arms in the village should be handed over under threat of death for failure to do so; several men surrendered weapons, but the Germans made this possession the excuse for executing them, along with other men found in the village. The women and children were herded into the church and

132

the men were then shot in the churchyard in sight of their families. many men escaped, however, because of their precautionary habit of sleeping away from home. The village was destroyed and every house burned; old and bedridden people who failed to leave their homes were reported to have perished inside. With the village in ruins, the women and children were marched away.

The Germans let it be known they would destroy every village in the area unless the people told them where the Bandouvas gang could be found; Bandouvas decided he could not be held responsible for any more grief and destruction and it would be best of the local people if he took his band elsewhere. Such a large group as they now were would also find it difficult to elude the encircling Germands.

A long day of waiting was spent in concealment. Then Dunbabin and the Bandouvas gang set off in the gathering darkness to return to the east of the island whence some three weeks later Bandouvas and his men were evacuated to Egypt. Another party turned their eyes westwards towards the high mountains; this comprised Fielding, Perkins, Pavlo Vernadakis, John Stanley, Ralph Stockbridge and his intelligence team, and their German deserter. Perkins and the others found the night trek a gruelling experience after little sleep and no food for three days; they had been keeping well clear of villages and it had been impossible to get food supplies. But the training in the Haifa camp some three months previously stood Perkins in good stead under these trying conditions.

The most dangerous part of their journey that night was near the village of Askyphou, site of the only easy crossing point of the road that led south through the mountains to Sphakia. German motor traffic was likely to appear at any time as the enemy were using the village as a headquarters for their raiding parties. If the group crossed the road together they would surely be seen; if they slipped across individually they risked losing contact with one another in the darkness. It was a case of 'boldness be thy friend'. They formed up on the road and tramped noisily in single file away from the bivouacked Germans in the hope that they would believe a patrol was on the move. The ruse worked, and soon Perkins and his companions were scrambling uphill on the west side of the road.

The sun was emerging from packed horizon cloud as they reached the main ridge of the White Mountains. Now, well beyond danger from German search parties, they made themselves as comfortable as possible among the stones and slept. It was past midday when they set off again, refreshed but hungry, yet thankful that in two days they ought to be back in the relative safety of their hideout in Selino. But events had taken a new turn in their absence. Before they had gone far they perceived their wireless operator, Alec Tarves, coming towards them with a guide. The demeanour of their approaching comrades foretold bad news and the story Tarves had to tell was to lead to a total change of plan for both Perkins and Fielding.

TEN
Epic of Koustoyérako

What are we waiting for, assembled in the marketplace,
The Barbarians are to arrive today.

— Cretan *rizitika*

Before the early autumn of 1943, the Germans showed little
interest in the rugged Selino region. But reports had filtered
through to the Occupation forces that activities against them were
being organised by British agents and Cretan guerrillas in eastern
Selino villages. To the extent that Koustoyérako, among the
highest of these, was the centre of the resistance in Selino, the Germans' information was correct. As was the case with many of the
upland villages in those days there was no road to Koustoyérako,
just a mule trail. And like many another mountain hamlet, its forty
small whitewhashed houses still wedge into the hill slopes; straddling opposing escarpments, they are separated by the village
square, a *kafeneion* in one corner. There are still no shops. Some
two hundred metres above, amid pines and olives, stands the tiny
church.

The track to Koustoyérako, about 750 metres above the fertile
Souyia valley, winds upward for seven kilometres and passes
through another village, Livadas. The present road and electricity
and piped water supplies are very recent innovations.

It is an area of deep ravines and craggy ridges. Above the village
are stony terraces of olive and almond trees, together with a few
crops which supply the villagers' food needs apart from their

135

sheep and goats and some poultry. Almost the only industry is the collection and bagging of olives to be sent to the oil presses, and with so little in the way of material possessions, the peasant style of living is largely unchanged. Intermarriage means that it is still a close-knit community, although some of its more enterprising sons moved away after the war to reap the benefits of modern commerce and living. What the villagers lack in wealth they make up for in spirit - a fiery independence pursued belligrently for centuries. Today, it simmers below the surface, ready to emerge under provocation.

With the Paterakis brothers as the core of the local resistance movement, the guerrillas enjoyed considerable success against German units sent into Selino to try to find and destroy them. The enemy operated in small in small groups and, although the Germans dug hides in the hills and waited in ambush, the guerrillas were expert in ferreting them out. The leader of one of the German groups, known only as Hans, proved himself more ruthless than others and was reported to have boasted that he had killed ninety-five of the guerrillas operating in Selino. He further bragged that if he caught the Paterakis brothers he would take them to Chanea and hang them in front of the central market place. It became a war between Hans, surname unknown, and the Paterakis family. On one occasion they had the chance to kill three Germans accompanied by a Greek policeman, but Vasili Paterakis took two men with him and sent a message to the Germans that they did not want to harm them and that they wanted only the man Hans. They told the Greek policeman that if they found Hans they would kill him for what he did in Selino. And they pleaded with the Germans not to harm the people of the village, or any of the other andartes, for the matter concerned only the Paterakis men.

On a night near the end of September, a messenger from one of the British agents came to the Paterakis home in Koustoyérako, warning that a large force of Germans was moving from Omalos and heading in the direction of the village. The Paterakis brothers and several of the guerrilla force left the village and went into the hills for the rest of the night. At daybreak they heard the sounds of fighting in the valleys below. German aircraft swooped overhead and began bombing the villages of Koustoyérako, Livadas and Moni as the guerrillas came down the mountain to join in the fighting.

Along the way Costis came across the bodies of two of his uncles - Niko Paterakis and Andonis Paterakis - brothers of his father, Yanni. As he wept, anger surged within him; it rises even today when he recalls the scene. Cretans climbing the hills to escape said that the Germans were killing indiscriminately; they mentioned the names of several people who were dead, and they told of Germans shooting women, teenagers and children. Costis sent a messenger to nearby villages asking for more men to join in the fighting before setting off with a dozen guerrillas determined to avenge the killings.

They came unexpectedly upon several Germans; with the advantage of surprise - although the enemy were only fifty metres away, the Germans had not seen the guerrillas - Costis split his force so that the attack could be mounted from both sides. The enemy were caught in the middle and it two hours of fighting six of the Germans were killed. Several escaped and hid in a valley behind Costis's position. In the skirmishing which followed several more Germans were killed, most of them by Costis. 'Only God knows how many,' he says, and he did it with a pistol, not a rifle, because they had run out of rifle ammunition.

The need now was to get bullets from the Germans because at that time the Cretans had German rifles. The guerrillas shouted to Costis to ask who should go down to try to get ammunition and Costis, still enraged over the death of his uncles, shouted back that he would go himself. He ordered the men to cover him as he made a dash down to a point near the German position. Then he signalled them to stop firing; he expected to have to deal with several of the enemy, but he confronted only one. Before the German knew what was happening, Costis had lifted him above his head and hurled him alive into a chasm. The guerrillas then replenished their ammuniition supplies from the dead.

Meanwhile, below in Koustoyérako, the women and children were being interrogated in an attempt to learn the whereabouts of the British group, their wireless and the guerrillas with them. Having failed to get any information from the people, the Germans herded them into the village square and preparations were made to execute them. Costis reached a ledge where he had the village in view some four hundred metres away. He could see children being gathered together in a group, and the activity looked ominous. Three Germans carrying machine-guns were in sight.

What happened next is one of the classic tales of the resistance. Costis raised his rifle, took careful aim and fired. One German dropped dead. Again he fired and hit a second German in the leg. Another German shouted to his comrades to retreat. More Germans fell dead from the guns of the guerrillas as the surviving Germans fled, leaving behind several rifles in their haste.

The women and children wasted no time. Some took to the hills, others ran down into the valleys. Later, Costis reached one of the places in the mountains where a number of the escapers had gathered. They knew that it was he who had saved them: his reputation as a fine shot was well known. When he walked in among them they called his name and shouted, 'Welcome, wecome!' At the time he was not sure what had happened, but learned that four women and a young girl had already been shot before he had broken up the execution squad. The news that the others had fled to safety, however, allowed all the anger and weariness inside him to disappear.

The inhabitants of Livadas and Moni were not so fortunate.

Those who had escaped death were taken were taken to prison at Ayia, near Galatas. More of the men of the three villages joined the guerrilla band of the Paterakis brothers and pursued the enemy soldiers. In skirmishes during the last two days of September the Cretans estimate they killed more than a hundred German raiders. Surviving Germans made their way back to their base at Lakkoi to tell of the debacle.

The Cretans knew this incident was bound to lead to savage reprisals - probably wholsesale destruction, the fate of many villages in the Amari and Lasithi districts to the east - so collected food and remained in the countryside. Women and children were settled in mountain hideouts, in caves, in the guerrillas' headquarters, and in the sheepfold and cheesehuts at Achlada.

It is thundering in Selino, it is raining, but it is raining bullets.
The Germans invaded the three villages. They burned Moni and
    Koustoyérako and Livadas.
The braves have arrived . . .

The Germans were not long in retaliating. On 2 October a large force descended on the three abandoned villages, systematically destroying every house by blowing them up, setting them on fire, and bombing from the air. Also destroyed was the church which Perkins had attended several times. (Burned frescoes have since been lovingly restored.)

Once before Koustoyérako had been destroyed by an invader - theVenetians, nearly five hundred years previously. This was in reprisal for the revolt of the Cretans of the eparchies of Selino. Sphakia and Kydonia. In 1502, they had refused to acknowledge the republic set up by the Ventian occupiers or to pay taxes. The rebels appointed their own administration in Western Crete with George Kandanoleon of Koustoyérako as their governor.

Kandanoleon tried to reconcile the two administrations by pro-

139

posing marriage for one of his sones to the daughter of the Venetian noble, Francesco Molino. The marriage contract was signed at the baron's house in Alikianos, merrymaking went on all day, the wine flowed freely, and by nightfall no Cretan was left standing.

The Venetians, some 350 men and a hundred women, feigned drunkenness. They were soon joined by armies from Chanea and Rethymnon. The Cretans were bound as they slept and made prisoners. Next day they were viciously punished. Some were hanged in the amrket place in Chanea; many were shot. Others were sent to the galleys. Kandonoleon's village, Koustoyérako, was razed to the ground. The armies then combed the region, killing other suspected *rebels and destroying more villages.*

Like their Venetian predecessors, German raiding parties moved into the hills to search for the fleeing villagers encountering stronger resistance from the augmented guerrilla force. As the German raiders flung their net wider they endagered the wireless station at Pytharaki. Corporal Alec Tarves dismantled his equipment and Vardis Paterakis helped him to hide it. With the others from the encampment he moved higher into the mountains. Alec then asked one of them to guide him across the mountain trails to bring news of recent events to his comrades. (Later the Germans found the Pytharaki camp and destroyed it.)

Alec and his companion had been tramping for only a few hours when they came upon Xan Fielding and his party. Reappraising the situation, Fielding decided against continuing to Selino. It was obvious that the district no longer offered a secure base; it had now become as dangerous as any area held by the Germans. Troops were moving east from Selino through the White Mountains; from the other side they were moving west. The British and Cretan group was in danger of becoming mincemeat in the operational sandwich.

In the mountains the island was noticeably cooling after the hot, dry summer. To move higher out of the grasp of the German patrols would lead to uncomfortable living in inhospitable eyries soon to be eneveloped in the first winter snows , away from sources of food. The best chance for survival lay in moving down towards the foothills of Apokoronas and seeking a friendly village for sanctuary.

Another problem was the size of the party. There were too many of them to move safely into any village household, so it was decided to split up. As night closed over the range and it became safer to move unseen, Captain (later Major) Ralph Stockbridge and his party set off east towards their old hideouts above Asi Gonia. Perkins, with Fielding and Alec Tarves, moved down towards the northern coast, aiming for the village of Kyriakoselia. It was well past midnight, when after walking without a halt they reached the home of Levtheri Kourakis and his wife Frosso, whom Perkins had met on his trek in August with Psychoundakis. The couple constantly stripped their larder bare to proviion agents and runners on thier journeys; Levtheri was still suffering from a wound received in a German raid and beneath his balck beard his cheeks were sunken - he was fighting a wasting disease. Perkins would not have guessed that Frosso was in constant pain from stomach ulcers had Fielding not explained that the smooth skin of her face, encased in the black headdress of Cretan elders, concealed a stoic resistance to ill health.

In spite of their weak condition, in true Cretan fahsion, the couple wanted the visitors to have the comfort of their beds while they would sleep on the floor. But with the Germans likely to appear unexpectedly Fielding was not prepared to jeopardise their hosts. Already they were in considerable danger because of their clandestine activities. Nor was Fielding going to risk the security of Perkins, Tarves and himself.

They went out into what was left of the night to climb to a cave where they were assured they would be safe. Levtheri and Frosso insisted they shouldtake adequate food with them and again it was a matter of the Cretans leaving themselves short in order to sustain those who were fighting the battle for them against the hated occupiers of their island.

Once installed in the cave, Fielding and his band discovered it was much too dangerous to leave. Day after day, German soldiers roamed the hills on endless patrols. Perkins suffered like the others from frustration, a sense of wasted time. On more than one occasion patience wore so thin that they nearly yielded to the temptation of taking and dicing with danger. Caution prevailed and eventually the Germans disappeared, their withdrawal possibly had something to do with the weather - it was beginning to break, the mountain air was becoming cooler and on the fringe of the Lefka Ori lay the first white dusting of winter.

Fielding was anxious to be in communication again with Cairo. Rather than risk returning to the Selino district and finding they could not retrieve the wireless set, he decided that he and Alec Tarves should go to Asi Gonia. There he fully expected that the set they had operated earlier in the year would be recovered in good working order from wherever the local mountain folk had concealed it from German search parties.

After the destrution of Koustoyérako and the abandonment of the Selino station little information about the refugees from the razed villaged had reached the British agents. Perkins offered to return alone to Selino to see how they were faring and to organise the guerrillas there for effective action against the enemy. Fielding had formed a high regard for Perkins' ability and had no he-situation in allowing him to do as he suggested. Effectively this gave Perkins his own command and the New Zealander relished the challenge. The expectation was that the Paterakis brothers would have no lack of recruits from among the many villagers who had lot their homes in the German raids and from these men and efficient fighting unit could be moulded.

It was the first real chance Fielding had had to give Perkins responsibilities where he could use his initiative. Having made himself useful in many ways Perkins had shown Fielding that 'more than any other NCO I had met he had the makings of a brilliant officer". In those two months the BRitish Commander had come to admire Perkins' quiet aura of self-confidence. To Fielding, Perkins appeared 'much like I imagined Lawrence of Arabia must have looked - blue eyes in a long, lean face, with a high straight forehead, the two parallel lines which aran from each cheekbone to the corner of a square jaw-line, forming the sides of an almost perfect rectangle; and in character, too, he closely resembled what I had read about the famous Arab leader. He gave the impression of being a man with vocation, and beneath his habitual silence, I could discern a terrier-like restlessness."

Upon arrival in Selino Perkins found the men from the three ruined villagtes living as small groups in several hideouts. There was no cohesion, no unity; the Paterakis brothers' small band had suffered in recent encounters with the Germans and was no longer capable of mounting a tactical operation.

Perkins collected together about 110 men and set about welding them into an effective force which swelled at times to nearly two hundred. Women and children were leaving their mountain and valley sanctuaries and were finding refuge in homes in neigh-bouring villages. The extensive activities of the Germans in the Se-lino mountains had petered out and their patrols withdrawn to their base. The dragnet cast in a rugged wasteland where no-one lived permanently, where roads did not exist and tracks were few, had been easy to evade for folk with the area mapped in their heads. Only a handful of unfortunates were caught.

The reprisals, carried out in such a sparsely populated district, had only strengthened the people's loyalty, courage and de-dication to resistance. The Occupation commanders apparently re-cognised the futility of trying to continue their intimidation of the population in eastern Selino in efforts to flush out the guerrillas, and they made no further sorties at that time into Selino villages.

Reoccupation and reconstruction of the wrecked Pytharaki camp was not considered desirable and Perkins set about establishing new quarters in the vicinity of the Achlada sheepfold. He was determined to ensure it would be adequate to withstand the depredations of winter as well as organising it as much on military lines as the circumstances would allow. The main requirements were tents, arms and food. No longer able to rely on village people for some of their supplies, Perkins planned to make his quarters completely self-supporting, his community drilled and trained to take the offensive against the Germans. To accomplish this he needed the unstinted confidence and co-operation of the *andartes*.

Late in October, Perkins, Vasili Paterakis and others trekked north-east over the mountains to the Apokoronas village of Kambi to meet Fielding. They discussed various matters concerning the reorganisation of the group and its role in resistance. Vasili Paterakis was still the natural head of the group, but Fielding then aked him if they would accept Perkins to direct their activities. Without hesitation, Vasili Paterakis replied firmly: 'Like a brother,' and embraced Perkins in the Cretan manner of devoted friendship.

At this time, ever-increasing supplies were being assembled in the middle East for agents in Greece, Albania, Italy and Yugoslavia, and Perkins resolved to get a goodly quota for his andartes in Selino. In order to give Cairo a comprehensive list of his needs, he sent a message to an I.S.L.D. intelligence unit manned by Cretans at a place known by local people as Tromarissa, on the northern slopes of the Lefka Ori, just above Zourva. A wireless there was in direct communication with Cairo.

Perkins' theory was that if the camp was properly organised and provisioned then this efficiency would be reflected in the martial conduct of his men. Most essential for the guerrillas' well being was food, and the air-drops ensured they had plenty to let them through mid-winter spells when they might not be able to move out of camp for several days. He was insistent that the arms, ammuniition and equipment were adequate. Supplies landing away from dropping zones sometimes found their way into unauthorised hands, in spite of a legend on every canister in Greek which said: 'If found hand this over to the Allied officers to whom it belongs.' But a few Cretans who discovered canisters would regard them as gifts from heaven and unpacked them, looking for food. And who could blame them in such trying times?

Shepherds occasionally made gifts to agents, who knew the goods came from the drops. Agents seldom castigated the finder, feeling it expedient to say nothing. But once or twice they unwrapped packages in front of donors to show them they contained not food but explosives which could have blown them up.

Nor did agents take action when a shepherd appeared in new army clothing and boots which had not been issued to him. They smiled to themselves whenever they saw women's yellow silk underwear - the material of parachutes - put out to dry with the washing. Distribution of supplies to *andartes* and their families was usually very carefully planned = even so, jealousy and squabbling sometimes resulted.

British officers in the S.O.E. operation in Crete acknowledge unequivocally that Perkins very quickly produced a resistance movement in Selino that surpassed accomplishments elsewhere in the island. Several ambitious Cretan guerrilla leaders had been prone to let their hearts rule their heads and engage in irresponsible actions which provoked the Germans into violent reaction against a defenceless civilian population. On one occasion Colonel Dunbabin saw Perkins and his men in action; 'and it was simply spelndid to see with dash he led them. [This must have been during the fighting at Tsilivdika early in October.] His men became a very good force and did extremely well in actions against the Germans. This was almost entirely due to Perkins' power of leadership and the gift he had for getting the best out of pople.' The *andartes*, Dunbabin added, were absolutely devoted to him.

And so were the people, the women and children. After they had lost their homes and had to live rough it was Perkins who saw that they were provided with food and clothing from the parachute drops he ordered, supervising the orderly distribution of these relief supplies, essential with the onset of winter. In effect, he became responsibnle for the lives of many hundreds of families and refugees, as well as for guerrillas, scattered over country where it was difficult maintaining contacts. Fort many Cretans, comings and goings were usually confined to adjacent valleys; often there were were family and regional feuds - sound reasons for not venturing too far afield.

It was a big responsibility for Perkins, a job done with complete success. The deep attachment which the Cretans felt for the man was due not only to his personal heroism - though courge is perhaps regarded as the highest virtue - but also for his devoted care for their personal needs and wellbeing at a trying time. For his humanitarianism âs much as for his bravery is Perkins still remembered.

The Cretans were his people and they regarded him almost with the veneration due to a god. They had, clothed and housed him in his time of need; now he was repaying his debt a thousandfold.

Much of this success was due to Perkins' personality. He transmitted his quiet confidence to his 'troops' and impressed upon his men the need for loyal duty to each other and the group as a whole in the interests of security. He did this without imposing the strict military discipline against which his nature rebelled, but with insistence on efficiency, particularly in the care and use of weapons. Remarking that Perkins had 'incomprehensibly' been denied a commission, Fielding said he regarded him as a brilliant soldier.

'I was grateful the authorities had shown their usual blindness,' Fielding added, 'they might have posted him elsewhere and I would have been deprived of his assistance.'

To the guerrillas Perkins soon became 'Kapetan' Vasilios - the title conferred only on Cretans commanding their unreserved respect as a *pallikari* leader. Vasili, as he came to be known - the English equivalent is Basil - is, as with many Greek names, an informal abbreviation: in this case, of the word meaning 'the King'.

ELEVEN
Outsmarting the Katsikia

This Cretan earth of ours, wherever you dig it,
You will find blood of heroes, you will turn up their bones.

— Cretan *rizitika*

Alpine skies in Crete are usually clear and sunny until December, but winter in 1943 came early. November was dismal. A grey celestial shroud cloaked the lefka Ori; white flakes waltzed in a bitting wind, cascaded onto chilled stone and froze until the upper slopes resembled milky spray-whipped sea.

Thanks to Perkins' arrangements for survival in such conditions, the camp was fairly comfortable, sheltered, tented and compact. Perkins now looked every inch a Cretan. It was several weeks since he had shaved and he had grown a beard and a moustache. In Cretan garb, black-turbanned, knee-booted and sashed, on many occasions he foxed the Germans into believing he was a Greek.

An article of Cretan clothing which agents found most useful was the heavy shepherd's coat. Out of doors, in caves and camps, they slept in them. The cowl protected the face from cold in winter; in summer it proved stuffy but had the virtue of being an impenetrable mosquito net.

All the Allied agents lived like islanders. Some carried this to an extreme, seldom washing and becoming filthy and verminridden. Most, however, used an opportunity offered to take coldwater baths in streams, stripping naked, much to the dismay of Cretans who felt it shameful to expose their bodies. When Cretans washed they would bathe the upper part of the body first with the bottom half covered, then they would wash the lower part with the rest clothed. Cretan shepherds on watch for people stealing sheep were always reassured if they saw a man take off his clothes and bath naked - they knew the stranger must be British.

Fielding left Perkins to his own devices. He had complete trust in the New Zealander and felt he had no need to visit his encampment or interefere in any way. Periodically, Perkins sent reports to Fielding by runner to keep him abreast of developments. These despatches allayed any thought that Fielding might have entertained that he was needed in Selino.

Life on the mountainside became fairly routine for a time and Perkins was pleased with his *andartes,* their bearing, their enthusiasm, their high regard for him and their almost unquestioning obedience. He admired their skills with the weaponry provided by the S.O.E. airdrops. Although the conditions were difficult Perkins can, with some certainty, be said to have revelled in the challenge facing him.

Politics, as far as Perkins was concerned, had no place in his operation - he considered his main energies should be concentrated on the effectiveness of his guerrillas in action and their security. Vasili Paterakis warned Perkins that the Communists would attempt to break up his organisation. Nevertheless, Perkins paid little or no heed to political developments in Crete, unlike Fielding earlier when General Mandakas was demanding official recognition for his Communist-led E.A.M./E.L.A.S. The emerging Communist influence in Crete, though gaining some ground in the island, did not attract sufficient support away from the Cretans' NationalæOrganisation (E.O.K.) for it to be a significant threat, and throughout the occupation E.O.K. remained the dominant political and resistance group.

Perkins took his men as he found them. If he had a failing, it was that he placed more trust in some men than they deserved. He apparently overlooked, or did not want to believe, that one or two occasional helpers, though outwardly and normally loyal and friendly, could owe a primary allegiance to a local left-wing boss who might or might not be dependable.

Communist leaders could never be relied upon for co-operation in resistance work - as the S.O.E. found to its cost on the mainland. Jealousy motivated their actions, each wanting to do his own thing, each fired by sheer personal ambitiion. Perkins distanced himself from this domestic infighting. The enemy, as he saw it, were unequivocally the German occupiers; he was convinced that most, if not all, of his men were Royalists wanting no truck with Communism.

Soon after Perkins' return to Selino, Vardid Paterakis took him to the place where he had hidden Fielding's radio when the Germans began scouring the mountains for it after the destruction of Koustoyerako and other villages. Vardis had buried it and had covered the earth with pine needles: eventually they found it, but the earphones were missing. When they were about to give up hope of finding them they were discovered hanging on the branch of a pine tree, to their great surprise and delight. Vardis says Perkins embraced and kissed him and told him that while the enemy might well have found the radio, they would never have 'see the earphones up the tree!.

The Germans still wished to demonstrate they were in control in Selino and from time to time they sent patrols of about twenty men into the mountains. Yet even after the destruction of the eastern Selino villages, the area was still more sparsely garrisoned than elsewhere. The purpose of the patrols appeared to be to establish a presence and to round up livestock for butchering, rather than to flush out the guerrillas who, when they met in encounters, were usually greater in numbers and had the advantage of local knowledge. When the guerrillas decided to fight rather than hide, they engineered to do so on their own terms. Often under cover of darkness, they would creep up on German positions and make lightning forways - not so much in harassment as to recover sheep and goats taken from villagers whose need for food sometimes led them close to desperation.

When the Germans ventured into the hills it was usually Vasili Paterakis who laid down the strategy for dealing with the threat. He proved expert in contriving to lead the enemy into a trap; he knew the mountains better than anyone else, and his skill in planning, combined with Perkins' military mind, contributed to the success of the skirmishes in which the guerrillas were involved.

In November of that wartime year the sheep, which always spent the long, hot summers in the high mountains, had not yet been driven down to the lower slopes as would normally have been the case. Koustoyérako men, as usual, had lived out the summer at their sheepfold and cheesehuts at Achlada, a place appearing on no maps, east of their village and west of the great Omalos plain. Here they pastured their flocks and made the soft white cheese known as *haloumi*. The cottage industry carried on there was the crucible of the villagers' meagre existence; sheep spelled wealth for these mountain people.

One reason why the sheep were still on the heights was that after the raizing of their houses, the villagers now had no homes to go to; another was that herding the sheep down the mountain would only make it easier for the Germans to confiscate them. So in spite of the colder than usual weather, the sheep were still there. Sorties to steal the animals were made by Germans based on the Omalos plain. Some of the sheep they stole would be traded for potatoes: Cretans would be offered back one of their own sheep for five kilograms of potatoes. Perkins had come to know Achlada well and soon he was to know it even better. He had passed that way several times and was at the air-drops there; the hutments stood in a shallow depression among rocks and stunted alpine growths, a gully that is bone dry in summer and deep in snow in winter.

Some three weeks after he began reorganising the guerrillas he needed to communicate again with Middle East Headquarters. Although the wireless set hidden by Alec Tarves had been recovered, there was now no operator to use it, so another journey to Tromarissa was necessary. Perkins could have entrusted a runner with the message, but he decided to go himself, taking with him Vasili Paterakis, Vasili's brother Andonis, Nikos Metocharakis and Theophanis Protopapas. It was a trip the guerrillas would make frequently in order to maintain contact with Cairo.

With the mission accomplished, the five men headed back on their journey to the camp. Upon reaching the mountaintop known as Galati they used their field-glasses to scan the surroundings for any movements indicating a German presence. On the heights above Achlada, at a locality known as Kalonaulimona, they spied a party of Germans resting. They could have only one purpose in being there - to steal the sheep roaming in the area of Achlada.

Perkins and Vasili Paterakis left the group to get a machinegun hidden with stores at Matomeni Plaka (Bloody Field), taking a route through the crevices of Avaratakia. They also wanted to let other members of the guerrilla band know about the presence of Germans in the Achlada region and to enlist their aid in attacking what might turn out to be a strong force.

Andonis Paterakis, Metocharakis and Protopapas stayed at Galati and kept a watch on the Germans' movements. After a while the trio saw some seventy sheep, belonging to Gregory Giorgiakakis, coming from the direction of Achlada, undoubtedly being driven by a German foraging party, and going towards the slopes of Mount Psilafi. By then it was beginning to get dark.

The three Cretans formed a plan of attack to recover the sheep. Protopapas was left at Galati with a Luger pistol and a hand grenade, having no rifle. Andonis and Nikos went down the mountainside and took up positions on slopes opposite the well of

152

Petrokourta where the sheep would go for water. By this time it was quite dark; the guerrillas could not see the Germans, nor could the Cretans be seen. But the pair lying in wait could hear the flock moving below. When they judged the Germans to be near enough, Andonis and Nikos began firing blindly in an attempt to terrify the enemy. Shortly they were joined by Perkins and Vasili Paterakis and several more guerrillas, firing from above, also blindly.

The ploy succeeded. The Germans abandoned the sheep, which were all recovered and driven to a place of temporary safety. Next day the guerrillas resumed their patrolling of the heights and protection of their flocks.

Another attempt by the Germans to steal the upland sheep was made a few days later. The incident - on 15 November - is still vivid in the memories of the men who took part. Vasili Paterakis, especially, remembers it well.

"We were at the hideout in the forest,' he says. 'We had two boys on guard on a height. They saw several Germans on the move, rounding up sheep, in the Psilafi locality. To alert us one shouted: "Oi tragoi erhontai ta katsitika (The goats are coming, the billygoats). "We never said "Germans," we always referred to them in this way."

About a dozen men moved out to attack the enemy. As they approached the area Perkins took Andonis Paterakis and three other young andartes and turned south. Vasili Paterakis and six others continued on and suddenly saw the Germans. They were moving towards Perkins' group, who were a kilometre away and were in danger of being surpirsed.

Vasili Paterakis' first instinctive reaction ws to call out to warn Perkins. But he knew if he did that he would alert the Germans to the presence of the other party. An uncle (killed in a later engagement) said to Paterakis, 'Ah no, Vasili (Perkins) must know, he must be aware.'

153

'How can Vasili know, Vasili Paterakis replied. 'He cannot see them on the other side of that ridge. We should alert him.'

After due consideration he decided to use fire. There were branches and ferns in abundance and he told his uncle to light some and to throw them in the air at the same time as he did.

Perkins saw the flames, realised their significance, moved his men up cautiously until they had the Germans in view, and opened up h his machine-gun. Vasili Paterakis' men also opened fire.

The soldiers - it was later revealed that three were Italians - left the sheep and took cover among the rocks, but they were caught by fire from two directions. Some were killed - seven, it is believed - and the survivors scrambled away. A number of them raced over the crest of the ridge surrounding the Achlada sheepfold and da-shing down the slope on the other side towards the mitato (cheese-hut), a strongly built two-roomed stone structure. Vasili Paterakis and his men followed in hot pursuit. He recalls: 'I said to the boys, "Let's encircle them when they get inside."

Meanwhile another group was being pursued by Perkins, An-donis Paterakis, and the men with them. The Germans stopped to set up a machine-gun on the ridge above Achlada and were taking aim when Perkins hurled a grenade. One German was killed and the others raced down to the cheese-hut to join their companions. Stampeding in, the Germans shut the door, made of stout wood, and piled tables and furniture against it to impede any attempt at entry.

Paterakis' men positioned themselves along the rocky rim. When Perkins arrived they spread out and the New Zealander set up the machine-gun. Their numbers increased as another party ap-peared. Steady fire was exchanged with the Germans, who were replying throught the hut window. At times the barrage was in-tense, but the guerrillas failed to make any impression on the enemy, who were well protected by their stone barrier. Machine-gun fire and grenades hurled at the door had little effect. At one point three or four of the men ran down and climbed onto the roof, but they were unable to do anything once there. Frustrated, the Cretans bided their time.

In the afternoon, with the Germans still secure in their fortress, Perkins became impatient. He decided to rush the door and try to force an entry. His men gave him covering fire as he ran towards the hut. Carrying a Bren gun, he approached from the side and shouted: 'Evga exo, Evga exo! (Come out, come out!)'

But the Germans were in no mood to surrender. They shouted back: 'Heil Hitler!' ! 'Heil Hitler!'

As Perkins moved towards the door, his weapon at the ready, Vasili valled to him: 'Get back, they will get you!"

A moment later, a shot was fired from the window. It hit the woodwork of the door, ricocheted, and Perkins was seen to stagger. The bullet hit him in the shoulder; he aborted his attack and rejoined his men.

'He was not scared,' said Vasili Paterakis.

Later in the afternoon, although his wound must have been giving some pain, Perkins led another charge on the hut, this time avoiding fire from the window. Again he shouted for the Germans to surrender and in response they asked for two of the guerrillas to go inside and negotiate a ceasefire.

Two of the men impetuously ran to enter the building, but Perkins, standing by with his Bren gun, yelled: 'You devils, come back, come back!'

The men who were willing to go into the hut expected that the Germans were ready to capitulate. Manoli Paterakis, recounting this, said, 'Of course, they could have held our people and made them captives. They could have used them as hostages until the Germans received reinforcements.'

The Germans shouted that the guerrillas must be running out of ammunition and would not be able to attack for much longer. But while the battle raged two of them were bringing hand grenades

155

and ammunition from the hideout 'by the sackful'.

Although Perkins' arm had been rendered useless he continued directing the attack while George kandanoleon and Nicolas Papadoyiannis were sent to find a doctor and bring him up the mountain. In the fighting which followed, Vasili Paterakis was wounded in the leg. Manoli Tsatsimakis from Ayia Roumeli rose boldy to fire at the hut and his rash act in thus exposing himself drew a shot which injured him.

Towards evening, one of the guerrilla fighters had a bold idea. On the side of the hut was a ventilator; if they could knock it out they could then throw in grenades. Some of them moved around and approached the hut from the side to begin battering at the ventilator: when they had made a hole in the wall they threw in a grenade. But the Germans were not fisnished yet. They pulled up a heavy table used for spreading cheese and placed it over the hole to stop the entry of more grenades.

Their resistance could not last long. Those still alive were all wounded, and they shouted out that they would surrender. The guerrillas ordered them to lay down their arms and come out with their hands up. Nine slowly emerged and were taken prisoner; inside, the guerrillas found four dead. The battle had lasted all day.

It was now five o'clock in the evening and the darkening skies accompanied a foretaste of the chilly night to come. It was considered unsafe to stay in or near the cheesehut and the problem for the guerrillas was where to go. First they collected the bodies of the dead Germans and dropped them into cavernous holes to prevent them being found by enemy patrols; their identity tags were kept to be sent eventually to Cairo. Then there was the question of the fate of the prisoners. The Cretans did not want to be burdened with them; they urged Perkins to dispose of them then and there - their own lives were at risk unless they were rid of the Germans.

Perkins was loath to agree. It was legitimate, he felt, to kill Germans in the heat of battle, but it was another thing to kill in cold blood: he had regard for the Geneva Convention on the treatment of prisoners, even if the Germans in Crete took heed of it only when it suited them.

The Cretans argued that in German hands they themselves would not be spared, so why they not kill the Germans? They were murderers not worthy of mercy after their destruction of villages and shooting of innocent women and children. But Perkins warned them they should not act like barbarians, as the Germans had done and the respect the men had for their leader prevailed - for the time being.

The Cretans led their prisoners over rock and shale to a cave a short distance away. It offered a safe hideout, its entrance well concealed. When Perkins' wound was examined it was discovered that the bullet had travelled down his back, lodging by a bone close to a kidney. There was as yet no doctor and the guerrillas had no medical supplies with them; there were no anaesthetics, nor was there anyone with even the remotest knowledge of surgery. Perkins realised that the bullet had to be removed, and without too much delay.

'Someone, even if he's a butcher, must do it,' Perkins is reported as saying.

He asked Politheros Kapourakis, who had cut up animals, to do the job, but the man was reluctant to tackle such a chancy operation.

Perkins needled him: 'Come now, haven't you ever killed a sheep?'

The Cretan demurred no longer and unsheathed his knife, the curved ivory and silver-handled dagger-type weapon still to be seen today in the belts of men who have been *pallikaria*. As Perkins gritted his teeth the man traced the course of the bullet and carefully, with a steady hand, cut it out. The grit showed by their leader impressed the guerrillas - he was, indeed, as hardy as they were.

There was no alcohol or other disinfectant to bathe the wound, but that did not matter - sepsis was unknown in these mountain regions where the air was fresh and unpolluted. The blood flow was staunched and the incision bound. Perkins told the men: 'You did well. Now I have discovered what brave men you all are. In future I won't need to ask who is good.'

He told the guerrillas to give attention to the wounded Germans; nothing was attempted that went beyond first aid. The prisoners slept trussed and the night passed without incident and in a familiar state of discomfort. In spite of his wound, Perkins was still very much in command. Under the crimson veil of awakening day he and his men emerged to plan their next move. The Cretans were still urging him to finish off the prisoners and he again denied them, sending off scouts to watch for German patrols. One of the scouts returned to report that a large force of enemy soldiers was trailing towards the Achlada area from the direction of the Omalos plain to the east.

The Cretans then insisted that he now had no choice, but to execute the prisoners - their own survival depended upon not being burdened with them. Plainly, the guerrillas' lives would be seriously at risk and Perkins reluctantly agreed to let the men have their way. With the German force steadily approaching but still some distance away, the captives were linked together with lengths of parachute cord. The region here is one of rockslides, precipitous chasms and deep potholes. After being led from the cave, the prisoners were forced to trudge to the edge of one of these holes, a cavern with a surface entrance. According to Vasili Paterakis the drop to the bottom was about twenty-four metres.

The idea was that roped together as they were, the first to fall would pull the bodies of the others into the pothole, but the plan went sadly wrong. After the first couple had been machine-gunned and dropped, their weight hauled the others over the rim before they could be shot and, still alive, they fell screaming to the bottom. This alone was not enough to despatch them and the guerrillas could hear moans coming from below.

In spite of the urgency of escaping from the approaching German force, Perkins was unhappy about leaving men suffering in the hole. There were also other considerations - if found by the enemy soldiers, the injured men could impart information hazardous to the guerrillas. The incident might also send the enemy on further rampages against innocent civilians.

None of the Cretans was initially willing to go down to put the men out of their misery. The cave had a bad reputation and the brave fighters were superstitious. Then Andonis Paterakis elected to do the job. Lengths of parachute cord were hastily knotted together and the others began lowering him in. He was only a short way down when the cave's evil genie acted - one of the knots slipped, the rope parted and Andonis crashed to the bottom.

From below came a shout: 'Oloi tha pethanome mazy! (We'll all die together.)' It was a German soldier.

One of Andonis' legs was injured and he was in pain. Perkins, though still suffering from his own injury, insisted he should be let down to rescue Andonis and to do the job Andonis was to have done. Andonis' brothers protested that it would aggravate his wound. But their leader asserted that he had a duty to complete the task he had sanctioned.

At the bottom of the cavern Perkins went about the business of administering the *coup de grace* to those Germans still alive. He then tied the injured Andonis to the lifeline and the Cretan was hauled to the surface.

How much Perkins suffered in being lowered to Andonis is not known, but there is little doubt that he must have been in great pain. It was an action again for which he is still remembered, contributing to the legend of 'Kapetan Vasili'. Andonis is said to have had an ornate ring that had belonged to one of the dead Germans, kept as a reminder of the events at Achlada. But later, in Cairo while he was playing football with English soldiers it slipped off his finger and was lost.

Although they were now unencumbered by the prisoners, Perkins' men were handicapped by the wounded in trying to evade the Germans hunting them. Mist settled over the high terrain and a persistent drizzle set in; the guerrillas retired to seek sanctuary in an area of ravines and caves known as Akonisia. In the next few days some two thousand German troops were to comb the area with artillery adn aircraft in an attempt to smoke them out.

TWELVE
Feast of St Catherine

Take the crest of the mountain and stone by stone mount
And every stone you tread, one more struggle count.

— Cretan *mantinade*

When the Germans reached the area they broke up into groups and started searching for the andartes. They found footsteps in the damp ground but they were unable to judge their destination; 'the place was precipitous and with much rock, which left no telltale prints.

Costis Paterakis was in Zourva during the Achlada fight and news that his brother, Vasili, had been wounded reached him there. Immediately he set off to find the guerrilla group.

'There seemed to be thousands of Germans scouring the mountains,' he says, 'and I had to circle around to avoid them. I took my time and eventually reached Akonisia where I discovered that Perkins was also hurt and my brother Andonis injured.

'We made a plan to have five andartes with each of the more seriously injured men. We chose sanctuaries in the rock cliffs to form a defensive triangle.

'Two of my brothers and three *andartes* were with one injured brother. I was among those looking after Perkins. In the third corner of the triangle was my father (Yanni Paterakis) and four andartes with the other injured brother.'

Meanwhile, the two men who had gone off the previous day to get a doctor had some difficulty in finding one. They went first to

161

Kamaria on the other side of the Souyia Valley; there, they were told that a doctor could be found at a cave known as Spilia. Eventually he was brought up the mountain and infiltrated into the hideouts. He cleaned the wounds, carried out such surgery as he was competent to perform in the circumstances, applied bandages and made the casualties as comfortable as possible.

From time to time faint guttural speech filtered through to the hidden men. Their expectation was that the Germans would give up at sunset and retire to their posts at Omalos and Lakkoi, but they reckoned without their enemy's Teutonic persistence. When night came it was evident that the enemy were still out in force; Perkins and the Cretans would not be able to emerge under cover of darkness and steal away down the mountain.

As far as they could judge, the Germans had made camp and were roasting goats they had killed over fires. It was late when the sounds subsided, and the thought of the enemy feeding on their own livestock only served to aggravate their growing hunger. They had but a few scraps of food; for water there were only the trickles down the limestone walls.

At dawn ears strained again, and soon picked up distant sounds of movement and of voices. All day the guerrillas waited for the silence that would allow them to come out of their dark and cramped quarters which must then have seemed worse than a medieval dungeon. The hours passed slowly; in the evening Germans were still nearby. For a second night Perkins and the Cretans gave up hope of leaving; cold, hungry and in low spirits, they huddled together for warmth and found it hard to sleeep.

The third day and night brought no relief. Sounds of revelry among the German campers only aggravated the discomfort of self-imposed incarceration. In such situations Perkins is remembered for strict fairness. One of his men, describing conditions in the caves, says Perkins was a pallikari *'filotimos'* (the word used to indicate a man of honour, a person who is proud and

162

careful of personal dignity, who can show self-respect and be generous and courteous).

'As on many occasions, we had little food. Vasili always had the same food as the others; never did he want to have a bigger ration. 'We were hungry, so hungry. We had only a kilo of dried beans and Vasili would hand out one bean at a time to each man. One man found he had a few crumbs of food in his pocket but he did not tell anyone, and only when it was dark did he scrape them out and eat them so that the others would not see his jaws moving. Vasili used to distribute cigarettes, but if he had only one cigarette he would pass it to everyone to have a puff.'

At one time the Germans were only twenty-five metres away, and the guerrillas prepared to fight their way out. They withheld their fire and the enemy never discovered how close they came to finding the hideouts. Costis says they could have attempted to drive them off by setting fire to the scrub, but luckily they moved away.

There are doubts about exactly how long the men had to spend in the caves before it was safe to come out. Many believe it was eight days but others put it at six or seven. What is apparent is that they had to spend about a week in vile conditions in near darkness, stiff with cold, stomachs cramped with hunger pains, a foul stench from their insanitary habitat assailing their nostrils. The prospect before them seemed to be death by starvation. Their fate if they gave up and surrendered to the Germans would be more certain.

Perkins' demeanour continued to earn respect.

'He was so calm, so cool, incredibly so,' said Vardis Paterakis. 'He could not be agitated easily; he was not afraid of death.'

Then a morning came when the men, now in a very sorry plight, noticed an unusual silence. The harder they strained to hear, the more convinced they became that the Germans had departed and that salvation was at hand. With feelings of great relief tinged even with exuberance though in no mood to dance a jig, they tested the situation, peering out and cautiously scouting the ground. They found that the Germans had indeed departed.

The enemy had feasted mightily and well on goat flesh. Where they had camped lay piles of bones, but they had discarded the heads and legs. Perkins and his men gathered these up and roasted them over a fire together with another goat they had killed. They ate ravenously while eagles circled above, sweeping down on what was left of the carcases.

'So hungry, so very hungry were we,' said one of the men. 'When the meat was eaten up we even ate the stomach with its contents.'

Thus sustained, the guerrillas were anxious to move down the mountain, but found they were still weak from hunger and exhaustion: Vardis Paterakis says his brother George walked only three hundred metres before he fell down. With what seemed a superhuman effort the group staggered on through rain. When they reached the forest they knew they would soon meet other comrades.

The rain ceased and someone asked what day it was. One of the older andartes said it was the Feast of St Catherine - 25 November. After their success in the battle and their deliverance from capture, the guerrillas felt that the gods had been with them; it had been a kind of miracle. Perkins told them after the war they must try to find a church in Crete dedicated to St Catherine and light a candle in thanksgiving for their escape.

'Now, every year, on 25 November, we celebrate the day,' says Vardis Paterakis. 'We take an icon and have a memorial service for those who lost their lives - Vasili of blessed memory, and about ten others.'

In one of the sanctuaries where women were sheltering, food was prepared for the hungry men. They told Perkins he should eat first. But Kapetan Vasili refused, ordering them to help themselves; he said he would eat when they were satisfied.

Wireless messages were relayed to Cairo, giving brief details of events and the identities of the dead Germans. In order to try to prevent the German garrison in Crete from launching reprisals against Cretan civilians, Cairo Radio gave prominence to the arrival in Egypt of German prisoners captured in the Lefka Ori by British agents and Cretan guerrillas.

Soon after the battle at Achlada, the sheepfold and cheesehut were reduced to ruins. The partial destruction brought by Perkins and the guerrillas was completed by the Germans with explosives. When a British motor-launch next came on a night voyage, Andonis Paterakis was evacuated to Egypt for proper treatment and convalescence for the leg injury he received in the fall into the cavern. Vasili Paterakis stayed behind in the mountain camp. He said he had drugs to put on his wounded leg - presumably sulphanilamide powder - and he soon became well. The other man wounded at Achlada, Manolis Tsatsimakis, was less fortunate. He needed hospital treatment but the Germans got to hear he was there, took him away, and put him in front of a firing squad.

Speaking some years later at the unveiling of the plaque to the memory of Perkins and Andreas Vandoulas, a prominent re-sistance fighter who is now president of the New Zealand-Crete Association in Chanea, Antonios Kosmadakis referred to the significant success of the Achlada operation.

'It was a perfect example of how a guerrilla force can beat an equal number of extremely well-trained and efficiently armed re-. gular soldiers who occupy the best strategic position.'

In his report on the killing of the prisoners, sent through Xan Fiedling on the S.O.E. base in Cairo, Perkins is said to have accepted full responsibility for the action taken by his guerrillas. One of the British agents who saw the report says the killing of the German prisoners was unfortunate, 'but it must be remembered that Perkins had no means of holding, much less of evacuating, prisoners at that time. It was just one of those stories of the brutality which inevitably occurs in time of war.'

Naturally the report was suppressed and still had not been officially released. Agents cannot say whether is still exists in the S.O.E. archives; in fact nobody seems able to locate the S.O.E. reports dealing with Crete. One or two sections of such reports which might touch on activities in the island are held at the Public Records Office in Kew, London, but they are closed for fifty years. Others have yet to 'come down', according to officials - presumably from the Ministry of Defence, which up till now has been remarkably unhelpful to researchers into British involvement in the Cretan resistance.

Perkins' account of the battle apparently did not fully tell of his principal role in the affair, and he made light of his wound. In the years since, the guerrillas with him have talked about what happened and the facts have gradually been assembled to be revealed here for the first time. Perkins' wound responded well to the doctor's ministrations, even though that gentleman appeared infrequently. He was obliged, he said, to report to the Germans every second day to give any treatment they needed, and if he missed doing so they beat him.

The New Zealander soon became well enough to turn his attention to establishing a camp on the heights above Koustoyérako, secure from the worst of the winter weather now setting in. Royal Air Force planes flew three missions to drop the supplies Perkins had ordered. Very little of these were lost; as well as food, they included books, small arms, ammunition, grenades and propaganda leaflets. But of greatest importance was the delivery of tents and winter clothing which were' to provide a touch of luxury for their winter quarters.

In reports to Fielding, Perkins said he expected to have no difficulty in holding out in Selino until the end of the war if airdrops could be continued. Fielding found reassurance in these statements and felt he would serve no useful purpose in visiting Selino. The British commander therefore concentrated all his attention on his own work in the rest of the territory for which he was responsible in Western Crete.

Every few days the Germans would appear on foraging expeditions, and with the same regularity the guerrillas would plan to get back any stolen sheep. They say Perkins had told them not to kill Germans unnecessarily if the sheep could be recovered without a fight. By moving quietly at night they often managed to do this without disturbing the enemy.

Vasili Paterakis and Perkins once accomplished this on their own. 'We were returning from the fields in the evening and we had no weapons except our pistols,' says Vasili, 'when we discovered some of our sheep missing. We found the sheep had been collected up the mountain. In darkness we circled around and, without trouble, drove away the stolen animals.'

There was another occasion when the guerrillas came upon a party of Germans with eight mules laden with food. The supplies could not be taken wihout a fight and an ambush was prepared. All the Germans were killed and the mule-train captured without loss on the guerrillas' side.

The Germans came to realise that a new leader was in the Selino mountains, and although they knew little of his ability and the strength of his band, they nevertheless put a price on his head. Only later did they come to understand the mettle of their adversary. A German officer captured later during the Occupation paid tribute to Perkins as 'the bravest man I have ever fought against.'

It was probably some time during the following weeks that Perkins met his lost of two years before, Manos Paroulakis, in whose company he had spent many nights in trees. In a letter to New Zealand, Manos tells how a rendezvous was arranged one night for some patriots to meet a party which would include an

'English officer'.

'We waited until midnight and you can imagine our over-whelming pleasure when it was Vasili who walked in.

'We fell on each other, our tears coupled with happiness. He asked all about us, about my parents, sisters and brothers. I asked him to come to our house, but he could not come at this time and promised to come later . . . but misfortune overtook him.'

THIRTEEN
The Elements and the Enemy

As much as I avoid fire I am burned by its flame.
My fate has ordered it, another is not to blame.

— Cretan *rizitika*

Just before Christmas Perkins received word that an S.O.E. motor-launch was bringing in an officer to replace Fielding, who was due to be evacuated for leave. On the night of 17 December Perkins and some of his guerrillas were waiting at the Kaloyeros rendezvous on the south coast to receive the new man - the same spot where Perkins had landed at the end of July.

The officer who arrived, Captain Dennis Ciclitira, though Greek by birth, looked every bit an Englishman. His father was Greek, his mother English, and the family had lived in London since the First World War. Dennis, with his public school accent, was British through and through. Perkins led the new commander back to the mountain camp above Koustoyérako; it was arranged that Captain Ciclitira would stay in Selino to await the arrival of Fielding and be briefed by him.

A week later it was Christmas and Perkins, Ciclitira and the guerrillas celebrated in fine style. Although the Germans had pilaged the houses and taken what livestock they could find, a few animals were still around and theCretan men would come down and kill any they could find. That Christmas Day the camp had pork and goat roasted on a spit. Some of the women of the ravaged villages, now living elsewhere, brought bread and joined in the festivities. There was also food from the air-drops Perkins had organised. A hogshead of wine appeared, and possibly Perkins repeated his remembered salutation: 'Brothers - bottoms up!'

Meanwhile Fielding had heard that his replacement had arrived. The news came to him while he was at Captain Dick Barnes' wireless station, north of the road between Chanea and Rethymnon. Though recovering from a slight head wound received in a incident with the Germans a few days earlier, Fielding was eager to hand over his duties as soon as possible. He intended to arrange his own departure from the Selino coast and to rest, while waiting, in the comparative safety and comfort of Perkins' camp.

In fair weather, the journey to the camp would take two or three days, but the outlook was discouraging for a trek over the mountains. Snow hid the trails, the cold was intense, and the air was heavy with a dank freezing fogginess. In his impatience Fielding disregarded these hazards: as he set out accompanied by Pavlo Vernadakis, rain was falling almost continuously and on the higher ground it fell as snow. The journey took almost two weeks, and Fielding was wet through most of the way.

Christmas Day that year for Fielding was one he would not want to remember, but which he would not soon forget. In a cave with Pavlo he shared a piece of cheese, *paximathis* (rusks) that were rock-hard, and a couple of onions. For drink they melted ice and snow. Lying stretched out on the cave's damp clay floor it was not easy to sleep, dog-tired though they were from struggling through snow on obliterated tracks. The white blanket deepened with every fresh fall, causing landmarks to vanish.

On New Year's Eve, Fielding and Pavlo staggered into Perkins' camp as dusk was falling, tired, cold, hungry, never so glad to find sanctuary and security among friends after a gruelling experience. It was the first time Fielding had met Perkins since October. The camp impressed him immensely and later he was to write: 'Had it not been for the arrangements Kiwi had made, we should never

170

have been able to survive in the conditions of heavy snow experienced early in 1944.

'The tents he had ordered . . . not only gave us protection from the cold but also instilled in their inhabitants, unaccustomed to such luxurious efficiency, a sense of martial pride and confidence. Our thin canvas walls might have been made of reinforced concrete, so impregnable did our position appear to us.'

The second day of January dawned grey and freezing, the air heavy with moisture. It was not long before the heavens released shredded white sheets. The fall went on all day and intermittently for some time afterwards until the camp was completely snowed in, making movement impossible. This gave Fielding time to bring Ciclitira up to date with events and to brief him on the current situation in the island, although the newcomer had full operational knowledge through his staff work in the preceding months in the S.O.E.'s Cairo office. (Later, Ciclitiria was to organise the May evacuation of Leigh Fermor, W. Stanley Moss and their supporting Cretans, along with the islands' German commander, General Kreipe, whom they had kidnapped; this is described in Moss's book Ill Met by Moonlight.)

When eventually a thaw set in, Fielding began making arrangments for his departure. Corporal Steve Gillespie, who had arrived before Christmas with Ciclitira as the new officer's wireless operator, used the wireless they had brought with them to send off the required message to Cairo. Fielding, now recovered from the exhaustion of his trip across the mountains, watched Gillespie plod through deep snow to reach the set, stowed away from the camp, and was relieved to think he would soon be on his way back to base.

With the snow sufficiently diminished for easier movement, Perkins organised a probe into enemy territory to determine their strength. After several days, during which they crossed the long valley celaving south to the Germans' guard post at Souuia, they reached the town of Kandanos, where one of the men lived.

Yanni Pendarakis, who was the group's quartermaster, took them to his home where he felt they would be safe. Somehow, perhaps through an informant, the Germans discovered the presence of the group. Perkins and the men left in a hurry and during fighting in the pursuit three Cretans were killed and Pendarakis wounded in his left shoulder. In order to speed their flight, Perkins and the remaining guerrillas lightened their packs by discarding their ammunition, and they got safely away.

Later, there were further heavy falls of snow; conditions in the guerrillas' hideout became almost untenable, the tents caving in under the weight of their thick white canopies. It was decided to move to the coast to a point on the mountains above Tripiti. At about the wireless message from Cairo which Fielding had been anxiously awaiting about his evacuation came through.

There also came a warning from Cairo, where German messages were still being deciphered, that on orders from Athens a big operation was being mounted to capture British agents and to destroy their wireless operations. Precautions and care were advised about the choice of sites for transmission and reception in order to remain in contact with base.

Food needed for the new camp was in store in the cave of Kaloyeros, opening into the sea, deposited there from one of the boat deliveries. Were they to go directly to the cave by land there was the chance that they might be observed by the enemy, if the Germans were in the vicinity. According to Vardis Paterakis, Perkins said it would be safer to swim around to the cave to reconnoitre the situation. If the Germans had discovered the store, Perkins said, they would be all around it and perhaps inside, waiting to pounce.

Perkins braved the cold sea and stroked his way towards the cave entrance. With no sign of Germans he swam in and found the store untouched. Emerging cautiously through the narrow landward entrance he confirmed that all was well. The party descended on the store to appease their hunger, collected some of the food, and humped it back to their campsite above Tripiti.

Now it was February, and Fielding felt the days dragging as he awaited his departute. Meantime, however, Perkins was not idle. As the German guard post at Souyia was so close to Kaloyeros, where the boat would come in, Perkins made a reconnaissance to ascertain what opposition they could expect if the mission was detected. At the bay he discovered that the post was manned by a German and five or six Italians. It appeared to Perkins that he and the men with him might have little difficulty in capturing the post. When challenged, the enemy soldiers made no attempt at resistance and surrendered. Perkins made them prisoners and took them back to camp. This was one of Fielding's last memories of Perkins - 'He had just captured a mixed post of Germans and Italians and was leading them triumphantly to headquarters.'

On the night of 9 February Perkins and some of his band guided Fielding down the mountain to Kaloyeros, along with the prisoners (who were to be interned) and a number of guerrillas who were to go to Cairo for rest and training. The motor-launch came in as scheduled and landed stores. Andonis Paterakis describes the cave as being at times almost like a warehouse, and already there were weapons and ammunition, clothes and foodstuffs, and a generator for electric lighting. He recalls that the German, and Austrian, was amazed at the cave and what he saw there and exclaimed to his Italian colleagues: 'Look, you see where the English are - and we were looking for them elsewhere!'

The embarkation - with Fielding among the happiest to be leaving - went without a hitch. He departed 'confident that so long as Kiwi was present, Dennis's mission in Crete would succeed'. Afterwards, Perkins and his men returned to the camp above Trtipiti.

It had all been very different from a previous occasion, when a motor-launch had come in with men and supplies and Perkins and the guerrillas had had to remain in the cave for a whole day afterwards. The *andartes* signalled for a long time by torch before the boat saw them; when finally it came in, a dinghy and a lifeline were used in the rough seas to land the cargo. The launch departed and the guerrilla group remained in the cave until daylight. When they prepared to emerge and start their trek to their mountain hideout they discovered that Germans were about. The assumption is that the Souyia guard post had seen the flashes or had heard the boats's engines. The guerrillas were all for making a run and a fight for it, but Perkins advised caution. 'He was lying down near the opening of the cave,' says Vardis Paterakis, 'lying as if sleeping, and he said to us "There are three Germans." And the Germans began moving down towards the cave, but Vasili never made a move. He repeated, "There are three Germans opposite us and there is nothing we can do."

'A young man in our group said the Germans could come down and find us, so we should move out and get away from them. But Vasili said: "Stay where you are and do not move." 'Perkins' caution paid off and after a day they were able to get safely away.

It appears that the operation against orders of Hitler. Although Crete had lost its military value since the defeat of Rommel in North Africa, his instructions were that the island was to be cleared of the British, some of whom were indulging in sabotage and harassment as well as collecting information. Hitler was hoping that when his new secret weapons had been perfected and were ready he would be able to use Crete as a base for recapturing North Africa, just as Crete was useful during the Germans' earlier drive into Egypt.

The Gestapo unit in Athens known as '3,000', in Pamissou Street, sent three experienced agents to Crete early in January to plan the operation with the local military leaders. They were a German officer named Werner Jacobi and two Greek collaborators, Andonis Krasopouliotis and Patroklos Filliatis. Jacobi had consultations with the local Gestapo chief, Lieutenant Bortman, and with the island commandant, General Borgiei. With the help of the collaborators Jacobi was able to gain knowledge of the mountain trails taken by agents around the ruined villages of Moni, Livadas and Koustoyerako, which formed a small cluster around the Souyia Valley.

Jacobi believed that constant watch on the movements of the agent s and guerrillas would uncover not only the wireless in the Koustoyérako area, but also sets in operation elsewhere in the island. A single sweep could then eliminate them all. This view was not supported by Lieutenant Bortman or Crete's commandant, who believed that if they waited, the agents and guerrillas would get to hear of the undercover exercise and disappear with their equipment before they had gained knowledge of any other wireless sets about which they did not then know.

At the end of January, General Borgiei invited Jacobi and Lieutenant Bortman to his headquarters in the villa which belonged to Venizelos in Halepa, Chanea, for the purpose of discussing strategy. He had very much in mind the severe mauling the andartes had given the SS security organisation led by Fritz Schubert, whose indiscriminate executions of innocent people and destruction of villagers had made him a marked man. Schubert and his force were ambusehd in the region of Meskla, suffering serious casualties and he managed to escape with only a handful of men. This incident greatly disturbed the Occupation heaquarters, but they considered nonetheless that they were dealing with only isolated pockets of resistance. This is evident from a midly-worded message to the Cretan people in the Occupation newspaper, *Paratiritis (Observer)* in which an appeal was made for funds to help the rehabilitation of those who had suffered in reprisals taken as a result of guerrilla activities. The villagers were also asked to cooperate in fighting communism and enemy agents.

General Borgiei also had information that new landings had

been made by British agents and commando units in order to undertake sabotage. He believed this was part of a much bigger plan aimed at eventually taking over the island, although he did not think an Allied landing was imminent. He had brought in radar to try and track down the wireless sets, but was hampered because the trucks on which the radar was mounted could not approach close enough to be effective since there were so few roads.

At the end of the meeting with Jacobi and Bortman, General Borgei gave his approval for an attack with a small force, prepared under cover of darkness for maximum surprise and mounted swiftly at dawn. Too large a force, it was agreed, would alert the British and the *andartes*. On the evening of 9 February, 1944, Jacobi and his men moved into the area around Souyia and Koustoyérako. The force was split into four groups - two to be used in the attack and two to be kept in reserve. German head-quarters was still under the misapprehension that no organised force of guerrillas now existed in the area after the departure of Bandouvas for Egypt. The truth was that the band led by Dudley Perkins was very much stronger than the Bandouvas gang.

Jacobi seems to have had information of the whereabouts of the guerrillas above Tripiti. To move against them he needed to go first by the coastal area at Kaloyeros and from three approach across the hills. Perkins' scouts, out watching for enemy mo-vements, and the Cretans' own intelligence system with in-formation passed on quickly by word of mouth and by shouting from hill to hill, made it easy for Perkins to prepare ambushes. And so it was to be this time.

On the morning of 10 February, some hours after the departure of the motor-launch, breakfast was being prepared over camp fires when Petrovasilis Harakis - who was on lookour duty - and Papas Haropapas came to the encampment to warn of a sizeabke force coming along the shore from the direction of Souyia. The

176

resistance men quickly stamped out their fires and packed their gear. Perkins and Vasili Paterakis mounted an ambush nearby at Kaloyeros where they knew the Germans must pass. meanwhile, Ciclitira, taking Pavlo Vernadakis as his guide, moved off to journey to his headquarters near Asi Gonia.

When his men were deployed, Perkins told them not to fire until he gave the signal. Soon the Germans were in the trp and he gave the signal to shoot. Perkins' own part in the action may seem foolhardy to some, but it is still talked about by those who witnessed it. Standing with a Bren gun at hip and pipe in mouth, he sent off burst after burst without cover of any kind while bullets whistled around him.

Brothers in the Paterakis family and Yanni Zambiakes were in the ambush and witnessed Perkins' behaviour. Ten Germans and two Greek collaborators were killed; among the many wounded was Jacobi, who was hit in the shoulder. None of the guerrillas was so much as scratched, though Yanni Zambiakes was lucky: a bullet hit his machine-gun, which deflected it.

The Germans then carried their dead back to Souyia and buried them there; with his reserves, Jacobi prepared to move againt Perkins' guerrilla band.

Meanwhile, Ciclitira was tramping through thick snow, travelling east. Costis Paterakis, who was with this group, remembers it as a slow, arduous journey carrying heavy stores and equipment which Ciclitira had brought with him from Cairo. Landmarks were cocooned in mist and the usual tracks proved difficult to find. What helped them to keep going was a good supply of cigarettes which the English officer had brought with him; their distribution helped to keep up the men's spirits.

In the next few days Perkins and his men engaged in skirmishes with the Germans, evading them when.this seemed the more logical thing to do. In the vicinity of Pikilasos, the group attacked a German party of greater strength, leaving two Germans and four

177

Italians dead and many wounded.

'Vasili was fearless; he had indomitable spirit,' one of the *andartes* declares, 'and he was contemptuous of death. He sat there on a rock, with bullets flying around, and someone pushed him from behind and he fell. Bullets were hitting the rock and Vasili was saying, "It doesn't matter, it doesn't matter,"'

As Perkins and his men were leaving the scene, one of the party, a well-known outlaw from Sphakia named Viglis, disobeyed instructions and fired at the Germans from an impossible range, the Germans retaliated and the guerrillas hastily took cover. In the exchange of fire one of the young Cretans, Rousos Zakimos, a Sphakiot, was hit, the bullet penetrating his chest. Perkins attended to his wound and when the fighting had ceased the party carried him away. Though seriously ill for a time (a Cretan doctor said he would die) the man survived under Perkins' care and was later evacuated to Cairo for treatment and convalescence.

The *andartes* then came upon a large body of Germans, said to number about 150. The guerrillas went to ground to wait and see what the enemy would do; eventually the Germans moved away and the guerrillas trudged on. For the comfort of the injured man the pace was necessarily slow. By nightfall, with mist rolling down and visibility limited, they reached Akonizia and its cave sanctuaries where food was now stored. There they spent an uncomfortable night. In the morning, cold and miserable, they were eager to be on their way to get the wounded man to a doctor.

Although the guerrillas tried to avoid meeting the enemy, there was a chance encounter in which George Paterakis was wounded, pinned down by machine-gun bursts from two directions. His comrades feared he would be captured, so Perkins and the others drew the fire of the Germans and allowed George to escape. Perkins is said to have claimed that had George not been wounded and needed to be extricated, they would have had a good chance to eliminate the whole group.

A day or two later, with the Germans still out in force, the guerrillas suggested to their leader that they launch an attack. Perkins told them that the risk was too great. Sitting on a rock, smoking his pipe, he said: 'No, my pals, it is not justified. A battle in which we suffer losses is not a victory. We should kill them, not they us.'

'He was surveying the scene,' one of them recalls, 'watching our soldiers and the Germans in the distance. We were about fifteen, and he was saying, "The devils, what good *pallikaria* they are." Some were saying to him, "Sit down, you may get hit by a bullet." But he retorted: "Never mind, bullets cannot kill from that distance."'

There were other similar occasions. Perkins would not allow his men to attack in situations when he felt they were likely to come off worst, especially when they were heavily outnumbered. Discretion was the better part of valour. Once when Varid and Costis Paterakis and two or three other men were in the high mountains with Perkins they came upon a lone German. The enemy soldier had not seen them and Costis raised his weapon to shoot him. 'Ochi, paidi mou,' said Perkins. ('No, my boy,') Let the soldier come to us, and when he is close we can jump on him and slaughter him quietly. If you fire your gun it will bring many more Germans here.'

At four o'clock one morning in mid-February, a party of guerrillas was in an area known to them as Mpaloma when they sighted Germans ahead at about the same time that the enemy noticed them. The Germans appeared to be waiting in ambush; in the gloom the guerrillas could see a machine-gun set up. They retreated hastily. Andonis Paterakis turned and fired in the direction of the enemy but there was no retun of fire. The *andartes*, who also included Yanni Zambiakes, took cover among pine trees. Then they began to wonder whether they had been imagining things.

179

In case they had not been mistaken, they trekked upwards, away from their original route. They had not gone far when they perceived enemy movements about a hundred metres away. Both sides began firing at the same time and an animated exchange went on for several minutes before the guerrillas withdrew. There were some close calls but no casualties, and they did not know what damage they had caused among the enemy.

The *andartes* then climbed toward a high range beyond which another group was camped. Two shots were fired to alert them that Germans were about and that they should leave. Hearing the shots, the guerrillas in the camp put out their fires, erased signs of occupation and joined Andonis' party. The *andartes* crossed a wide shallow valley to a point where they could observe a cave where Perkins and two more guerrillas were sheltering, lest Germans should appear there and make a search.

By then it was daylight and they kept guard until it was seen that the enemy were moving away down the mountains. Perkins and his companions emerged from their hideout in safety and went off to a hidden food store to bring back supplies for hungry men. Afterwards they headed for the lower slopes of the White Mountains in the north where small villages of the Apokoronas region lay at the ends of rough roads or tracks. Here the guerrillas knew they would receive a welcome. They rested, grateful for a short period of idleness after their arduous days in the high altitudes.

Refreshed with fresh food from the villagers, the pary then set off for their old stamping ground above Koustoyérako. As a refuge, they descended to the cave called Nerospili, a little over a kilometre from the ruined village. They hoped it would be safe enough, although it was low down the mountain, and that the Germans might have abandoned at least for the time being, their drive to ferret out the *andartes* and their Allied organisers. The Germans had indeed withdrawn - but they were formulating other plans.

FOURTEEN
Trail to Stefanoporo

The fire that lightened me shines no more upon me.
A wind extinguished it and now the darkness is upon me..

— Cretan *rizitika*

Soon after Captain Ciclitira reached his headquarters near Asi Gonia he found he needed a battery for his wireless set. He also decided to move his operations to another site near Kyriakoselia, in the Apokoronas area, and it was there he would set up his wireless. He sent a message to Yannis Vandoulas in Nippos to send a strong man to Selino to get the equipment he needed. When Yannis received the note, his brother Andreas was anxious to know what was in it. Yannis passed the note to him, and Andreas immediately said he would go.

Writing of the last time he saw Andreas, Yannis said he watched him leave 'through the ravines while snow was coming down. My brother had to walk about twenty hours through bad and dangerous tracks.'

On the way, Andreas went through Zourva and called on George Tsirandonakis. Andreas told George Tsirandonakis. Andreas told George of the planned journey and asked him to go with him to Koustoyerako. The two men then went to a place where a group of partisans wre camped and there they were joined by a third man, Panayiotis Tsamandakis.

They wasted no time and in two days reached the Koustoyérako area and delivered the message to Perkins at Nerospili. The time

181

they took for the trek was normal during good weather in summer, and exceptional given that winter conditions made the going much tougher.

Meanwhile the Gestapo agent, Jacobi, still smarting under the punishment meted out to his forces by Perkins' guerrillas, was determined that he would not return to Athens and admit defeat. He saw his chance to hit back when Leieutenant Bortman received a message from a Greek of uncertain loyalties about Perkins' intentions. Jacobi and Bortman accordingly made plans to deal with the people who had been humiliating his forces and causing serious losses among German patrols.

'We shall ambush them, as they have ambushed us,' Bortman is reported as saying. He told Jacobi he had picked out a suitable place above Lakkoi, where German guards had seen many people suspected of being andartes going through Stefanoporo, described as being near a waterhole at the end of a steep hillside, and near where there was a cave which the Germans felt sure was being used by guerrillas for shelter at night. Through the efficient Cretan 'bush telegraph' the information that the Germans knew of Perkins' journey not surprisingly reached the ears of Perkins' men.

Two incidents are cited by the guerrillas still living in Koustoyérako as indicating that attempts were made by communists to find out the movements of Perkins and his *andartes*. According to Vasili Paterakis, two men who were left-wingers, presumably communists, had come to the camp and had asked if the men there knew who had given the order for 'the Englishman' to be killed. The visitors were presumed to be guerrillas from another group, but Perkins' men did not know them. Vasili says he had not met them, and 'the boys' had not thought to ask who these men were. They were said to have stated that a man wearing a yellow shirt had approached them and and asked about the route the party with 'the Englishman' would take.

Another story, said to have a bearing on the circumstances, is recorded in the book Operation Crete, produced recently by Antonis K. Senoudakis, one of the men who took part in the abduction of the German General Kreipe. Senoudakis says that he was provided with a guide to go from Zourva to Achlada, but that this man 'turned out to be more of a traitor than a guide.' On the way, a shepherd shouted at him: 'Reh koumpare, reh koumpare' (a commonly used form of friendly address to a person one does not know personally or by name). Cretans have an inherent suspicion of strangers, and during the Occupation all strangers were suspect.

'Reh koumpare, I am not asking you where you are going and who you are. But you are unknown here. What are you doing here? There are Germans up there!'

When he received no reply, the shepherd pulled out a pistol to kill the man. But someone with the shepherd told him: 'Don't foul or dirty your hands.'

The shepherd is recorded as saying: 'I wanted to kill him, but I let him go. And he went off. I did not ask his name. Anyhow, he would not have told me. He would have rubbed his nose and his hands saying he was shy to see men;' (an idiomatic expression indicating he would not reply, or would have given an untrue answer).

The shepherd said he reported the encounter to the andartes' camp but nothing was done about it. His meeting with the 'stranger' took place a few days before Perkins set out on his last trek. In retrospect, the incident may perhaps be taken as based more on suspicion than having any factual relevance.

The Cretan say that Kapetan Vasili was warned about the possibility of betrayal and of possible danger from communist factions. The communists were jealous of the strength and success of Perkins' guerrillas and they were resentful that most, if not all, of the Selino *andartes* were staunch adherents of Crete's own National Organisation, while their own leader, General Emmanouel Mandakas, had failed to gain the official recognition of the British, thus rendering the communist less efffective in their common aim of driving the Germans from Crete.

'Our people were strong and powerful,' says Vardis Paterakis. ' The communists thought that if they could destroy our leader the guerrilla group would be broken up.'

The men with Perkins persistently cautioned him that he should not go on the trip, that he should not go on the trip, that he should not allow himself to fall into a trap. Others would deliver the battery. But Perkins dismissed this advice.

The group offered to make up a large force to go with him; about fifteen, they suggested. But still Perkins made light of the danger.

Vasili Paterakis, effectively Perkins' second-in-command, then said he should accompany his leader. Costis also wanted to go. 'I said we would go together,' Vasili Paterakis recalls. 'But he told me, no, you should stay here with the boys.'

It was Apokreo (the time for feasting before the start of Lent) and Perkins told them to slaughter lambs, to roast them and have a *glendi* during his absence.

'But we did not slaughter lambs,' says Andonis Paterakis. 'Instead we cooked beans.'

On 27 February Perkins set out for the coast to get the battery from the cave stores for Ciclitira's wireless. As well as Vandoulas he took the pair who had accompanied Andreas to Nerospili - George Tsirandonakis and Panayiotis Tsamandakis - and Yanni Zambiakes from Koustoyérako.

'We marched out in darkness,' says Zambiaikes, 'and I saw a woman all dressed in black who said to us: "Where are you going? You must not go."'

According to Greek folklore, if you see a woman in black, or a priest, and they presage something unpleasant or give a warning it is considered a bad omen. Zambiakes says the experience unnerved him. Somewhat apprehensive, he took the precaution of taking an additional weapon and extra ammuniition. 'I took a German pistol in addition to my Italian pistol and a hundred bullets instead of the usual fifty. I was worried and I feared that something might go wrong.'

The group also acquired a wireless set from somewhere, as well as the battery. One set had been found by Vardis for Perkins upon returning to Selino in the autumn; there was reported to be another said to have been abandoned by the wireless operator, Steve Gillespie, on leaving hurriedly from the Tripiti camp on 10 February. According to the guerrillas, the Germans discovered a set and took it away. It appears Perkins' group may have found the other and, as Perkins had no wireless operator, it may be that he decided to take it with him, believing it to be of more use elsewhere.

They camped that night at Tripiti and next morning, 28 February, Perkins and his five companions trudged off in fitful winter sunshine to climb over the White Mountains from the south to the northern slopes in Apokoronas. Perkins also had with him some 200 gold sovereigns, each of which was worth many thousands of drachmas, such was the state of inflation.

It was five days after Perkins' twenty-ninth birthday.

The group skirted the Omalos plain where the Germans had guard posts and dropped down to the north. As they were on the heights above Prases they heard a shot. Climbing to a point where they could observe where it came from, they saw two Germans descending towards a small house. The Cretans wanted to kill the Germans, but Perkins told them to desist. They were not going the way the party wanted to go, and attacking Germans was not part of their present mission. In any case, at that time it would have been unwise to attack Germans excpet in self-defence because the Occupation forces had rounded up some 500 Greeks from several villages and any attack on Germans might provoke them to shoot

185

some of these villagers in reprisal.

They continued their journey in the general direction of Zourva, to the east of the Germans' garrison village, Lakkoi. About six hours after leaving Tripiti they reached an encampment where there were more than 150 guerrillas. With them was a brother of Panayiotis Tsamandakis, Nikos, a Kapetan. While Perkins' group was resting, a party of German and Italian soldiers came into the gathering, led by a Greek acting as a guide, and entered into firendly conversation with Nikos and some of the *andartes* - possibly in an attempt to discover Perkins' movements. It was quite common to see Italinas with the Germans, as many Italians had been forced to join with German uinits after Mussolini's capitulation and the departure of the Italian commander in Crete. Some were also with the guerrilla group; consequently there must have been times in clashed when Italians were called upon to fight their own people.

When the Germans had gone, Nikos took Perkinsægroup into a remote part of the mountains against the possibility of the Germans returning in force. Then Nikos is said to have gone to Zourva - a small settlement of a dozen houses straddling a saddle in the mountains above Meskla - with the apparent object of procuring a guide t o take Perkins by a safe route because of the greater than usual presence of Germans. The guide was to be Dimitri Tsirandonakis, brother of George Tsirandonkais, but he failed to reach Perkins before the group moved on. (A report in the official war history that bothe Tsirandonkis brothers were with Perkins and escaped is not borne out by information available in Crete.)

The trail Perkins took led down into a rocky ravine with sutnted growth on one side and mainly rock outcrops on the other. In soft earth, fresh footprints were detected. Perkins told the others tht if they were not the prints of Cretan andartes then they must have been made recently by Germans, but he was assured that they were the prints of æour people'.

Nevertheless, one of the men who had been leading is said to have been doubtful and was hesitant about moving on, Perkins is reported to have remarked: 'Are you afraid? Then I will go in front.' It was British practice in the Cretan resistance tht group commanders should never lead from the front, but Perkins is said to have consistently disregarded this directive.

When the group had tramped on further a shot was heard. Zambiakes says he told Perkins there must be Germans ahead. But Perkins is said to have replied he thought they would be the *paidia* (boys) they were due to meet in the vicinity.

Moving on again, they began to climb the hillside of Stefanoporo.

Zambiakes, suspicious and on the alert, suddenly shouted: 'Germans!' He started to run back, but the others said it would be all right, they would be 'our people'.

As he hesistated, a voice said: æKomm! Komm!'

In that instant Zambiakes knew he had not been mistaken. They were Germans. In his opinion it was *prodosia* (betrayal).

There is a suggestion that the Germans were hoping to take the group alive, but they apparently perceived that their adversaries were not disposed to surrender. They immediately changed their tactics and decided to shoot first before Perkins and his men could use their weapons.

The Germans were deployed in strength - Zambiakes estimates about fifty of them. Perkins, out in front, had a Bren gun. 'Vandoulas and I had pistols,' says Zambiakes.

Before Perkins could use his weapon the first machine-gun burst from the enemy struck him across the chest. From his throat came a great cry: 'Voyithi!' (Help!). They were his last words. He fell back and was dead when he hit the ground.

Vandoulas, dashing to get behind a rock, was hit in the leg. He had been walking immediately behind Perkins.

Zambiakes, carrying a sack with wireless equipment, dived for cover.

George Tsirandonakis, who had a machine-gun, had no time to fire before he was wounded, fell over a ledge, and disappeared from sight.

Tsammandakis, who also had a machine-gun, faced with the intense enemy fire, leaped into a shallow crevice to escape the hail of bullets. But he was not quick enough and a bullet hit him in the stomach.

The closest Germans, according to Zambiakes, were only fifteen metres away. He tossed Vandoulas a bandage for his leg wound and both kept firing with their pistols. Zambiakes killed the German firing the machine-gun and another soldier. Vandoulas was hit a second time, the bullet tearing at his neck, yet he continued firing and shot dead a German walking towards him. The rock he was sheltereing behind did not offer the best cover from the spread of the Germans' fire. He fired several more pistol shots before a third bullet slashed into his head and killed him, his body rolling down the slope.

After that, the whole of the Germans' fire was directed at Zambiakes. From all accounts he must have had a charmed life and his escape after holding a vastly superior enemy force at bay for some three hours seems little short of a miracle. During the late afternoon he was able to keep the Germans pinned down; any who showed themselves had a psitol shot directed at them. He had no fear, only a passionate rage which he expressed vociferously, hurling inults at the enemy.

Then one of the German bullets found its mark and Zambiakes was wounded. It might have killed him, but a bag on his belt took the full force of the impact and the bullet embedded itself in his stomach.

Meanwhile, a Cretan in the vicinity, Evangelos Tzatzenmakis, became aware of the group's predicament and raced off to a nearby village to try to get help. Earlier, for some reason, Perkins had changed clothes with Tzatzemakis.

In spite of his wound, Zambiakes kept up his harassment of the German. 'Altogether I killed five Germans,' he relates. (He perhaps hit five; only three bodies can be attributed to him.) 'The Germans were trying to get me, and as the sun was setting they were firing to the right and to the left of my rock cover. With the sun low, the long shadow of one German shooting at me made him seem very close - only two and a half metres away. Then God's evening arrived and allowed me to slip away.'

Incredible though this story seems, it was later confirmed by German sources to a British agent.

Zambiakes made a painful getaway, crawling through the ravine. Shortly he found Tsamandakis who had managed to crawl away and lie up. With him was George Tsirandonakis. When he toppled over the ledge he survived a heavy fall and had hidden in a gully, later to crawl away and join Tsamandakis.

The three took some time to stagger in darkness to a hiding place where there were people who rendered first aid. Patriotic Cretans helped Zambiakes through the night and as day was breaking, he reached the house of Papadomanoli, in the village of Karanos, not far from Lakkoi. There he was given shelter. Village people heard of his arrival and came to find out what had occurred; the Cretan grapevine had it that two men had been killed in the mountains.

One story that seems to have the ring of truth is that Perkins was expecting to spend the night with a guerrilla leader in the area named Kyanis Kyanidris. Earlier, the Germans are said to have routed Kyanidris and his men from their hideout on their way to set up the ambush. They had thus eliminated a possible source of opposition to their plan. And for once, the usually efficient Cretan communications network had failed to convey a warning to the travellers.

After the German force returned to its post at Lakkoi next day, it was caimed that they had killed four guerrillas. A team of forced labourers was sent out to recover the bodies. They came back with six - four Germans and those those of Perkins and Vandoulas. The labourers were directed to dig graves near the Germans' quarters, close to the road near the north-eastern edge of the village.

The Germans at first believed they had killed Evangelos Tzatzemakis, a much wanted man with a price of twelve million drachmas on his head. This was because the Cretan's papers were in the pockets of the clothes Dudley had exchanged with Tzatzemakis.

After the burial of the two men - one report says they were accorded military honours - villagers kept the graves constantly covered with fresh flowers without molestation from the garrison. When the Germans left in October 1944 to concentrate around Chanea, the Cretans planted flowers and cypress trees on the graves and whitewashed the stones surrounding them.

There Perkins lay until after the war when his remains were removed to the Commonwealth War Cemetery at Souda Bay. The headstone on his grave records his death as having occurred on 25 February 1944 - the date which appears in his official records at the Ministry of Defence in Wellington - but Cretan historians and officials insist that the fatal ambush was three days later, on 28 February. That is the date engraved on the plaque erected on the road near Stefanoporo in 1971.

The final resting place of Andreas Vandoulas was in the cemetery of his village, Nippos, alongside the graves of his fore-fathers and relatives.

The people in Karanos who were looking after Zambiakes sent a runner to inform Perkins' guerrillas at Nerospili about the failure of the mission and to seek help for Zambiakes. Several of the *andartes* came over and in a trek over fifteen nights, hiding by day, they brought Zambiakes on a makeshift stretcher to sanctuary near the ruined village of Moni in the Souyia Valley. There, local people took care of him and three doctors arrived to give him treatment. 'The wound had worsened,' says Zambiakes. 'It was smelling: it was a long time before a doctor attended to it.'

Arrangments were made by radio for a motor-launch to come in for an evacuation of wounded for treatment in Cairo. It was 23 April when it arrived _ nearly two months since the encounter at Stefanoporo. Zambiakes was taken off, along with Tsamandakis. Yanni Pendarakis, who was wounded in an earlier incident, was among a half-dozen others who went aboard the craft at Tripiti. George Paterakis, determined to go with them, stowed away after several times being discovered and put ashore.

When Zambiakes was fully fit and well - although his wound left him with only kidney - he joined the Sacred Greek Regiment of commandos, led by an English colonel, and served in Italy as a parachutist.

What a tim Charos has chosen to take you.
Now when the branches are blossoming and the earth
*   putting out grass.*

- *rizitika* for the death of the hero Diakos, 1824

FIFTEEN
Was there Treachery?

The Sphakian mountains cry, central and Psiloritti,
Because the Germans slaughtered the bravery of Crete.

— Cretan *mantinade*

British agents concerned with the Cretan resistance are sceptical that treachery was involved in the death of Perkins. Some admit it is not impossible, but Xan Fielding expresses 'total disbelief' in this theory. And for the S.O.E. records (and they are not available for perusal) it is believed they assumed that Perkins' encounter with the Germans was by chance. However, S.O.E. men are ready to agree that the Germans might well have heard of Perkins' journey and were out looking for him. Harokopos, in The Fortress Crete, quotes German sources for his conviction that Perkins' group walked into a carefully prepared ambush. The original intention might well have been to capture Perkins and his men alive – there are reports to support this – but it seemes that when some of the group attempted to escape, the Germans opened fire.

The region around Lakkoi, where the German attackers were based, had a small but close-knit group of communists - the town was the home of General Mandakas - and those remaining in Crete after he went to E.L.A.S. headquarters on the mainland were still smarting from the snub by the British in not according them official status. There was therefore sufficient incentive for them to try to cause the disintegration of groups under British official recognition and organisation. Perkins' group was undoubtedly the most competent and successful fighting unit among them, and to destroy it would be a significant blow to British operations, leaving the communist groups in a more favourable position to lead resistance in the island. Certainly, too, a few individual communists favoured the Germans rather than the British, in spite of the Nazi attack on Russia.

The finger of suspicion has been pointed at several people by individuals and groups, both verbally and in published reports. These have led to charges of libel; those who have been named as betrayers of Perkins have vigorously denied the allegations and some of them have named others in defence of themselves.

The web of doubt, disbelief, accusation and condemnation has been spread wide; it has enmeshed people who can be proved conclusively to be completely innocent. Stories have been embellished in the retelling; lamentably, they sometimes emerge in print. Facts have been twisted and misconceptions perpetuated to the extent that widely held beliefs, which have been proved to be completely inaccurate, persist in the minds of some people more than forty years later.

One instance: in some quarters it is firm belief that Perkins' mother came to Crete after the war to meet the men with whom he fought in the resistance. The truth is that Mrs Perkins did not go to Crete. She remained in Christchurch, receiving letters from several Cretans who loved and admired her son. The only close member of the Perkins family who has been to Crete to meet Dudley's companions in the resistance is the youngest brother, Neville, and his visit was not made until more than thirty years after the war.

A common Greek concept is that nothing is ever simple. Greek scholars advise cognisance of this in weighing evidence. Undoubtedly, something in the nature of a witch-hunt, pursued with almost the zeal that characterises the traditional vendetta, has taken place. Several resistance men are firmly convinced that

Perkins' death was engineered by leftists, jealous of his success – that they betrayed Perkins to destroy his organisation and to strengthen their own standing in the eyes of the local population. They say the evidence is that leftists were seen fraternising with Germans near the place of ambush a short time before Perkins' ill-fated encounter and that they were also with Germans at houses they were using as a base.

Another factor which could have influenced a betrayal was the sizeable quantity of gold sovereigns Perkins was carrying - wealth and currency that spelt easy living for its possessors at a time of want. Some of this gold might well have been promised for information.

Whatever happened, the incident has led to feelings of hatred, developing in strength with the passing years, as false stories hardened into misconceived convictions.

Xan Fielding says lack of security - an endecmic fault in the loose-tongued Balkans - is more likely to have been the cause. The small number of traitors in his area, he says, were virtually all known to the British agents, and they had already dealt with most of them.

Destruction of Perkins' group, however, was almost accomplished. The guerrillas' grief was intense; without the leader they loved and admired they went to pieces, separating into small groups. Although while in mourning they did not entirely cease operations, they were largely ineffective.

Manoli Paterakis had gone to Cairo shortly before Perkins' last trek and he heard the news of his death there. S.O.E. told him he should return to Crete and reorganise the disintegrating group; Manoli was only a month in Cairo before he was landed back on the island to perform that task.

'I found that the men had split up,' Manoli said, 'but I managed to collect together about 105 of the andartes and they still had their weapons. I stayed with them for a while until I received or-

194

ders to leave.' That was when he went to meet Patrick Leigh Fermor, who had landed earlier elsewhere to organise the kidnapping of General Kreipe. manoli led Leigh Fermor's Cretan helpers in capturing the Geenral, secreting him out of the island and taking him as a prisoner to Egypt.

Vasili Paterakis, who wanted to accompany Perkins, says he would never have gone by the route through the ravines. He would have kept to higher ground, which was normal practice.

The only other S.O.E. man in Crete to be killed was a Coldstream Sergeant-Major, Bill Knox. This occurred about eight days after Perkins was killed. There was no apparent reason: the deed was not done by Germans and it was thought he was murdered for the gold sovereigns he was known to carry for defraying expenses. His radio was also stolen.

The Perkins family was not told of Dudleyæs whereabouts while he was on special operations in Crete. They thought he was in Cairo; all mail to him was routed through the Egyptian capital to the care of his cousin, Captain Jim Bain, who in turn passed it on for delivery through an S.O.E. contact.

In Ministry of Defence records in Wellington there is a blank from 29 July 1943, when Perkins' promotion to staff sergeant was noted, although the promotion was probably made earlier, until 25 February 1944, when it was recorded that he was 'killed in action in Crete' - a date the Cretans say is incorrect.

All the details about Perkins' S.O.E. operations in Crete are held by British authorities. Officially they are 'not available'.

Perkins died beofre he knew the outcome of the Patarakis' vendetta against Hans, the ruthless Gestapo NCO. While no doubt in sympathy with the emotions of the Paterkis men, Perkins _ humantitarian though he was - would have recognised he was in no position to deter them from a centuries-old tradition that prevailed still, war or no war.

The final act that sealed the fate of Hans took place in May, several weeks after Perkins' death, when members of the andartes group of Vasilios Paterakis and Nicholas Metoxapakis learned that Hans was in the village of Temenia, a few kilometres to the north-west of Souyia. An ambush was laid, and Hans paid the ultimate penalty for deeds that had wrought so much havoc to life, property and passions of the close-knit community embracing Koustoyérako, Livadas and Moni.

Men believed to have been involved are reluctant even today to talk about the attack: it was, they say, a personal matter - an issue between the senior *andartes* and the man who, alone, was deemed the insigator of the destruction of the three villages and of the heinous deaths of several honourable people who were shown no mercy.

SIXTEEN
A Soldier and a Gentleman

Who is born in the world and doesn't know strife
Is a stroller that passes and doesn't know life.

— Cretan *mantinade*

Both Dunbabin and Fielding recommended Dudley Perkins for the highest award for bravery, the Victoria Cross, for continuous and exceptional gallantry and leadership. Earlier, after the Achlada attack, Fielding had also made a recommendation for an award of the Distinguisehd Conduct Medal for gallantry in action. This, he said, 'unfortunately did not come through in time,'

Fielding had great admiration for Perkins. 'Kiwi was the bravest man I have ever had the honour to meet,' he wrote. 'He was one of the most delightful companions imaginable. He soon proved himself a born guerrilla leader. His coolness in all sorts of sticky positions and his tremendous dash in attack - which I witnessed personally on many occasions when we went into action together - earned him the profoundest respect and admiration of the Cretans whom he knew and loved so well.

'None of the responsibilities, dangers and discomforts ever damped his spirits,' Fielding added. 'Every note he wrote to me was full of enthusiasm and good cheer.

'I am sure he met his death in the manner in which he himself would have not preferred - at the top of his form, utterly happy in the glory and violence of battle and in the certain knowledge that his activity was a major contribution to the cause for which he fought and died so passionately. It was then that he was recommended by me for the Victoria Cross.'

What happened about these recommendations is uncertain. They may be somewhere in British archives, gathering dust in a Ministry of Defence vault in Whitehall. Certainly nothing came of them. Unofficially, several reasons have been given why Perkins' exploits were not much more suitably recognised - the strict requirements governing the award; the fact that those actions meriting recognition were not witnessed by a British officer; that the nature of the mission, classified as secret, could not be revealed in any citation.

Major T.B. Mitford, who also said Perkins 'deserved this supreme honour', added that 'he had no chance of getting it because the exploits have to be witnessed by senior officers and I fear there is not other posthumous award a man can get. As the great Vasili, he is already a leading figure in the legends of the liberation of Greece, an honour to his country.'

It was more than ten months after Perkins' death before any official statement acknowledged the great work he accomplished in Crete. This was merely a 'mention in despatches' in the London Gazette of 4 January 1945. No details were given.

From all the evidence, Perkins was totally absorbed and completely happy. For the first time in his life he was able to use his ability and resources to give full value. From October 1943 until his death at the end of February 1944, Perkins evidently drove himself constantly to the limits of endurance. The strain was physical and mental, pitting himself against both the mountains and the enemy as he had set himself against Rendel in the hills of Palestine. He made the pace and he more tan took his share of the chores, lugging the supplies and carrying the wireless equipment. He asked no more of his men than he was prepared to do himself, and he was constantly mindful of their comfort and health.

When food was in short supply he would not eat until their needs had been satisfied, and sometimes he would go without when he felt others were more in need.

Apart from the responsibility of planning at the military level he had the interests of the men's families to consider. He saw to it that they received as much care and protection as his military children.

Marika Lagonikakis, who lived at Neo Chorio, some distance from Perkins' sphere of operations, tells how the fame of Kapetan Vasilios had penetrated as far as her village. At that time she was an impressionable girl of sixteen and she and several of her friends of similar age left their village on a trek over the mounship, but their desire was to plead with him to send them to Egypt for training so that they could return to join his organisation. He had become a legend in his own time. The girls failed in their endeavour to find him and not until many years later, then married to Ian Begg in Christchurch, did Marika learn by chance that he was a New Zealander and a Christchurch man to boot!

Time has dimmed the memories of many of the Cretan resistance men about events during the German Occupation. Details numbers and dates are often disputed among themselves, but their memories are crystal-clear when Dudley Perkins' role in their operations is discussed.

Undoubtedly, this man from Christchurch made an indelible impression on them, a tribute to his quietly assertive personality whose strength lay in a strict code of gentlemanly British conduct moulded by his clergyman father and supportive Christian mother. What strikes the listener forcibly is the complete lack of any adverse criticism of Perkins' activities and behaviour - apart from the lament that he took unnecessary risks and failed to listen to them when they advised caution, suspecting treachery on the day he was killed. They remembered the minor indiscretions of other agents, but for Dudley Perkins they found no fault that irked

199

them in any way.

The word *pallikari* elevates Perkins to the level of their top fighting men. To describe him as a *filotimos* (a man of honour) crowns him yet again. In the words of Antonios Kosmadakis, at the unveiling of the plaque to the memory of Dudley Perkins and Andreas Vandoulas in 1971, 'Vasili' is revered as 'the greatest New Zealand soldier of World War Two and one of the outstanding heroes of a long an bloody fight for independence and freedom - fearless leader of a band of guerrillas which became a major nuisance to occupying Germans.'

The story has become intertwined with myth. Schoolchildren recount his exploits; he is mentioned in their books. To utter his name in *kafeneions* often leads to the charging of glasses with that fiery spirit, *raki*. And in the hills, where his memory is still strong, there are echoes of songs about 'the brave Kapetan Vasili'.

Perkins' commanding officer at the time of his death, Dennis Ciclitira, says Perkins was offered leave and rest in Cairo, but that he did not want it. (It was intended that he should leave the island when Leigh Fermor took General Kreipe as his priosner to Cairo.) Perkins, he said, had come to regard the mountains as his home, and he thought that if he took leave he might not get back among his Cretan friends. 'I felt he had been there too long,' Ciclitira added, 'that he had become part of the furniture.'

Another indication of his desire to stay was given in one of his reports to Fielding before Ciclitira arrived, when he wrote that he expected to have no difficulty in holding out until the end of the war if the air-drops could be continued. Ciclitira says it was typical of Perkins' behaviour that he felt any risks should be taken by him. A scout should have been sent out ahead on his last journey, and on the trail it was custom that the group leader should not travel out in front.

Other agents have paid their own tributes.

Colonel Tom Dunbabin: 'What he did in Crete was really

200

worthwhile, and few men could have done it. He was one of the bravest men I have ever known. It was like him to be in the leading party, in the post of danger.'

Corporal Steve Gillespie: 'Dudley was worshipped by all who knew him and commanded a greater respect from them than anyone else I knew, including British officers.'

W. Stanley Moss, author of *Ill Met by Moonlight*, who did not himself meet Perkins, wrote: 'Borth Fielding and Patrick Leigh Fermor felt for him something like hero-worship.'

John Stanley: 'No other member of an Allied mission was loved, respected and admired as was Kiwi. He has grown into a legend that will never be forgotten.'

And from members of the guerrilla band came numerous lamentations and praise.

Michalis Tsirandonakis: 'His courage in many instances brought us through many dangerous episodes. His fame in Crete is great and to us his name will forever remain inmortal.

'Even to those who only heard of him, he was a hero, and they wanted to meet and acknowledge him personally.

'He was put in command of our camp and the wireless operation and I was an officer under his command. He planned to bring us food and clothing - in which he succeeded - and by this means we were able to go patrolling behind the enemy lines to collect information and send it to the Middle East, and certainly it was very dangerous.

I used to take the patrols to friends' places and have a meal before returning to our group. We very often nearby clashed with the Germans, but we tried avoid them. They would be many and we were only a few and carrying wireless equipment. But when we went into battle with them, it was always Vasili in front and giving us encouragement.' (Tsirandonakis here gives a glimpse of the guerrillas' role not mentioned by others - the gathering of intelligence for Headquarters in Cairo.)

Yanni Zambiakes, who was with Perkins when he died: 'Such a *pallikari* he was, such a *pallikari* has never been seen before, so brave was the New Zealander, he of blessed memory. No better *pallikari* can be found - not even among Cretans who claim to be *pallikari*.'

Vasili Paterakis, head of the six brothers forming the core of the Koustoyérako resistance: 'Vasili (Perkins) was a sound, very sound, brave *pallikari*, with youthful manliness . . . we were together for two and a half years. It was a sin for him to be killed unjustly. This man should have lived, he was worthy of life. He was a capable man, a pity to perish.'

Andonis Paterakis calls him a 'rare *pallikari*, indomitable *pallikari* who had not been spoiled by wickedness, cunning. He was so pure and innocent that he could not imagine that there could be betrayers, traitors and informers.'

Vardis Paterakis said the guerrillas all wept when they heard he had been killed. 'My mother (Eleni Paterakis) cried for him as if he were her own son, so popular, so lovable he was. He was a loss, a great loss, for us all, for all the village, a great blow. To us he was like a brother, such was the esteem we felt for him.

'He was so polite. Whenever he called someone he never used his name but would address him as *paidi* (a term of endearment for a boy): "Paidi ela do (Boy, come here)." When he was out and people saw him they all admired him and used to say. "Here he is, here he is!" My mother loved him like her own child.

'His loss was a heavy blow, deplorable. Everyone wailed. He used to say to the boys: "When the war is over we'll all go to New Zealand." How sad he's gone. He perished unjustly.'

Manoli Paterakis says: 'He was a sound *pallikari*, brave, robust. No-one has declared that he was not a good, brave man. We valued him.'

And this from another: 'He was fearless, with indomitable spirit, contemptuous of death, *filotimos*, a very sound *pallikari*.'

202

Vardis Paterakis remembers how, three weeks later, Perkins' death was brought home to them again. It was the arrivalæof mail from Cairo for British agents and from Cretan friends in Egypt. Included was a parcel from Perkins' mother for Dudley. 'It contained canned fruit and sweets,' he says, 'and its arrival from a mother to her dead son revived the grief we felt. We all wept again.

In the spring of 1944, S.O.E. was stepping up its operations in Crete, sending more officers and men. Had Perkins survived, the likelihood was that he would have been commissioned in the field, as were some of the British NCOs.

Major Jack Smith-HUghes, who controlled the Cretan Section of S.O.E. for most of its existence, says the fact that only two men were lost on operations in the island shows how lucky the group was, 'and how unlucky poor Kiwi was, but then he took more risks.'

EPILOGUE

Mother, should my friends come, should my brothers come,
Do not tell them I am dead, for they will weep.
But spread the table, give them food and wine,
Spread the table, let my brothers sing.
— Cretan *folksong*

For many years - and even today, as the authhor found - when the resistance is mentioned in the company of Cretans, almost the firs name recalled is that of Kapetan Vasilios. Among the older generation Perkins is still remembered with great esteem. Most of the statements by men of the resistance recorderd in the last chapter were made in 1985 - forty years after the end of the war.

From time to time, flowers still apppear on his grave in the Commonwealth War Cemeterey on a gentle slope overlooking Souda Bay, although clumps of geraniums grow there permanently.

Five years after the war there was a touching tribute. Photographs sent to the British Consulate in Chanea showed a small girl about to lay a wreath on Perkin's grave. Its inscription read: 'Grave of the most fearless of fighters ever to leave New Zealand, known to all Cretans as the famous Kapetan Vasilios. Killed over 100 Germans single-handed during the Occupation. Led a guerrilla band, and fell from machine-gun fire in February 1944, near Lakkoi - the last gallant Kiwi killed in Crete. This man is honoured by all Cretans.'

The accuracy of the statement that Perkins killed over a hundred Germans single-handed' is questionable. So far as is known, no tally of the numbers killed by the guerrillas, either before or oafter Perkins organised them, was kept. The probability is that during the time Perkins was with the guerrilla band they collectively accounted for something approaching the number of Germans attributed by some unknown person to Perkins alone. The legend of Vasili has not dimished with the years; rather has it been enhanced, and it is understandable that at time some Cretans are given to exaggeration. As Fielding points out, Perkins also captured several prisoners; where it was possible, they were sent into captivity in Egypt.

The war changed the lives of many of the highland villagers. For generations they had shepherded sheep, made cheese from the milk of sheep and goats, and tilled stony pieces of land on the mountaun slopes to grow grapes and nuts and vegetables. During the Occupation the Germ,ans commandeered most of the animals for their own use; the few they left for the villagers were often stolen by raiders. Many were given willingly to agents, guerrillas and stragglers. The end of the war thus saw scarcely a sheep left on the island; the mountain dwellers were deprived of their traditional livelihood. Upland villagers moved in large numbers down to the towns, seeking the means to live and a new kind of life.

George Psychoundakis has laterly been tending the graves of Germans soldiers in the cemetery on the hill overlooking Maleme airfield; he has not retired but returns there one or two days a week. After the war he was jailed as a deserter because of a bureaucratic muddle in which his war service papers were lost. Then he had to serve two years in the Pindus Mountains in Macedonia in the civil war. He returned to Asi Gonia to find his family in dire poverty, taking a job as a navy on a road being built up to his village. Eventually he had to leave Asi Gonia to avoid being caught up in a blood-feud; for a time he eked out a meagre existence as a charcoal burner in the Sphakian mountains. Today he has a neat house on the main road in Tavronitis, to the west of Maleme, where I found his daughter typing the latest manuscript of his extensive writings.

The village of Koustoyérako has changed little since the prewar days, and life there is barely above subsistence level. Yet the 150 or so people are happy and enjoy the mountaun conditions. Some forty of the destroyed houses have been rebuilt, most on the foundations of the old, but a few alongside the original dwelling, leaving the ruins as a reminder of that day in 1943 when most of its people narrowly escaped death. The village square is flanked by a kafeneion where any day of the week can be seen the village men discussing local affairs over innumerble cups of the thick, syrupy Greek coffee. Opposite is a stone-walled, burned-out ruin, a monument to German depredations.

Above the scattered houses olive and almond trees flourish on walled terraces. Among the thyme there is the hum of bees bringing nectar to numerous hives. An occasional tinkle of a bell betrays the presence of lambs and goats. Koustoyérako lies about 750 metres above the Souyia Valley and the first access road was roughly hewn only a few years ago. In 1985 this was greatly improved, properly graded and partly sealed.

As the young folk grew up they moved to the towns while the older villagers stayed. A few of the homes, still furnished in rough country style, have the modern miracle of television.

Yanni Zambiakes, who was with the Perkins when he was killed, still lives there. After much wrangling with the authorities in Chanea he was awarded a small war pension. He was 19 when he fought with Perkins; 71 in 1986.

Of the other survivors of that ill-fated trek, George Tsirandonakis returned to his village of Zourva and is now dead.

Panayiotis Tsamandakis was sponsored for emigration to New Zealand by a Dunedin man, Graham Davidson. Arriving in Dunedin in 1963, Tsamandakis first took employment in a meatworks. Later he moved to Wellington and pursued a trade as a carpenter. He lives with his wife and son in Palm Avenue, Kilbirnie; as his command of English has remained fragmentary they interpret for him. His younger brother, Dimitrios, lives close by, and a thrid brother, nikos, lives in Athens.

In Crete, the Tsamandakis family lived in Meskla where, according to Panayiotis, they sheltered eighteen stragglers at various times, including Milton Knight of Auckland, and Gordon Davis of Wellington. The Germans destroyed the family home because of these clandestine activities.

The distinguished Paterakis family, proud and unbowed, lost all their sheep and their livelihood. After the war, when their home was in ruins, the British gave them the keys of the German stores to take what they wanted. All they took was an iron bedstead - nothing else. The brothers found work, mainly in Chanea, always returning when they could to their cherished village. Vardis, who walks with a limp - the result of a wartime leg wound - has a house there, as has Costis. George settled in his wife's village of Azoyires.

For many years, Vasili Paterakis, 76 in 1986, has run the Pikilasos Hotel at Souyia, helped by his wife, Prokopia, Souyia a tiny south coast fishing village, its beach fringed with scrawny tamarisk trees, is seven kilometres from Koustoyérako.

Manolis Paterakis, who joined British agents in capturing General Kreipe, was offered a passage to New Zealand in recognition of the family's help to New Zealand stragglers. But he stayed on in the rebuilt Koustoyérako; the health of his wife, Eleni, precluded emigration. While favouring the life of a shepherd, Manolis was forced by necessity to work at Maleme aerodrome, at the factory of Demos and as a gardener at the German cemetery. He retired to Koustoyérako where he told me he had no regets about not going to New Zealand, pointing to the rugged beauty of the steep slopes rising high above the village. He walked with the aid of a stick, yet still went hunting in the hills. On 16 November

207

1985, he shot an ibex *(agrimi)*. Running towards the animal, he tripped over his gun and fell over the cliff of Toumba to his death. He was 73. Patrick Leigh Fermor - the man who masterminded the kidnapping of General Kreipe - and George Psychoundakis were among the among the many former resistance people who attended his funeral.

Andonis, Costis, Vardis and George these days often meet in Chanea with other resistance men, Pavlo Vernadakis, Antonis Kosmadakis and Manousos Manousakis and are ready to chat, if asked, about those stirring times. And at weekends, the Paterakis often gather in their old mountain village. Vardis says when he goes hunting in the mountains he often passes th eold hideout and remembers the magnificent oven which Perkins built for cooking and the amusement with which the Scots wireless operator, Alec Tarves, greeted the contraption.

In Koustoyérako, the name of Kandanoleon still exists. Georgios Kandanoleon, who wa one of those who fought with Perkins, is a descendant of the man from the village who nearby 500 years ago was put to death by the Venetians when he attempted to reconcile his Western Crete administration with the invaders. (See chapter 10, 'Epic of Koustoyérako').

In the nearby village of Livadas, German youths and girls made a visit some years after the war and built a community centre for the villagers in atonement for the depredations of the wartime occupiers. And in the ton of Kandanos they installed water pipes where none existed.

Sklavopoula, where Perkins spent Christmas 1941 at the home of Iphigenia Papantonakis, is still the sleepy little village it was then. When I visited it recently its small clutch of whitewashed houses and three churches, strung along a mountain ridge high above a deep valley, appeared deserted. Adjacent ground was tilled and vegetable crops were thriving. Yet, in half an hour there, I saw not one person. It was late morning. The kafeneion was

Above: *A group of villagers, some of them former resistance fighters, outside the kafeneion (coffee shop) in the centre of Koustoyérako.*

Below: *The village of Koustoyérako.*

*A plaque commemorating Dudley Perkins and Andreas.
Vandoulas, photographed on the occasion of its unveiling in
1971 by Antonis Kosmadakis, president of the Crete-New
Zealand Association (pictured).*

*The inscription reads: "1600 metres to the place Prinoseli
(Stefanoporo) where the Germans, in the clash of 28 February
1944, killed the fighters of the resistance Andreas G.
Vandoulas and the New Zealander Dudley Perkins (Vasilis).
Your death is an example to us. Your fellow fighters of the
resistance 1941-1945."*

The hill of Stefanoporo, in the middle distance, which Perkins had begun to climb when he was ambushed and killed. He had trekked down the ravine in the foreground.

The grave of Dudley Churchill Perkins at the Souda Bay Commonwealth Cemetery.

Nerospili, the hide-out from which Perkins left on his last journey. In the picture are Neville Perkins (left), Yanni Zambiakes (right) and his son.

Above: *A typical pallikari in his native dress and headband, as still worn today.*

Above right: *Two of the most prominent resistance fighters in Selino - Pavlo Vernadakis and Costis Paterakis.*

Right: *Georgios Kandanoleon, of Koustoyérako, one of the guerrillas in Perkins' band.*

Left: *Tom Moir in the Western Desert, 1940.*
Right: *Perkins with Gunner Nash at the artillery observation post at Pinos Gorge, Greece, in April 1941.*
Below: *Dudley Perkins (right) on a night out at Tel Aviv in January 1943 while on an officer cadets training course. Others in the photograph are, from left, Don McKinnon, Max Marsh, an unidentified officer and Jack Dawkins (above).*

Dudley Perkins, photographed outside his tent while with the 4th Field Regiment in the Western Desert.

Vasili Paterakis with two British agents, Lieutenant Peacock and wireless operator Corporal Steve Gillespie.

Two of the principal guerrillas of Koustoyérako - Vasili Paterakis, proprietor of the Hotel Pikilasos at Souyia, and his brother Andonis.

closed, so was the tiny market. Not a dog, a hen or a cow was to be seen. On the way down the rough, stony road to the next village, Kalamios, the only sign of habitation was a shepherd driving his sheep up the mountain to new pastures on bare hills.

Iphigenia (usually known as Fifi) is now Mrs Griggs. She lives in Harbour View Road, Onerahi, an honorary member of the New Zealand Crete Veterans Association. This honour was accorded her in recognition of the help she gave stragglers and escapers in Crete, feeding, clothing and housing some twenty-five men. As well as Perkins they included Jim McDevitt, Ned Nathan, Ken Little, Dave Cutherwood, Ned Phelan, Bill Rolfe, Joe Stratford, Bella Johnson, Bert Gill, John Kerr, Len Mitchell, Tom Moir, and Erci Owen. After the war she married Captain Ron Griggs, of 19 Battalion, when he went back to look for missing persons' graves. They returned to New Zealand and Ron Griggs died in 1985.

Ktista, where Perkins went in the late autumn of 1941, is still not served by a road. Only a track gives access, a few kilometres from the now rich tomato-growing area of Koundoura - hectare upon hectare of plastic-covered frames housing hundreds of tons of ripening fruit.

Elafonisi, one of the gathering points stragglers seeking boats, is still remote and desolate with no permanent habitation. It is the haunt of campers, hikers and sailboard enthusiansts, accessible by car to those willing to crawl along a treacherous road formed more by traffic than official roadmakers. The island, home of Mediterranean bird life, can still be reached by a knee-deep paddle of a couple of hundred metres.

Previli Monaster, destroyed by the Germans, was after the war. Representatives of the Allied forces returned to Grete on a mission of thanks to the people who gave aid to stragglers and special agents.Britain presented to the restored monastery a pair of silver candlesticks in appreciation of the monks'loyalty to the Allied cause; an illuminated scroll signed by the Prime Minister of New

Zealand, Peter Fraser, and by General Freyberg hangs in one of its rooms.

The original monastery, now in ruins on a lower site was founded nearly 400 years ago. The present church, centrepiece of today's monastery, dates from the nineteenth century and has distinctive frescoes and ikons. The church's greatest treasure is a gold Miraculous Cross in which is embedded a fragment of the True Cross - credited with the cure of many human afflictions.

When the Germans pillaged the monastery they stole this Cross and attempted to sell it in Crete. Failing to do so, they tried to take it to Athens. But the plane with the Cross aboard would not rise on its take-off run. When the Cross was removed the aircraft had no difficulty! Taking this as a sign, the Germans returned the Cross to its rightful place. Once before, in 1823, the Cross had been stolen. it was taken by Turks, occupiers of the island for 300 years. Later, a Genoese ship was halted inexplicably off Rreveli in spite of fair winds. The monks learned that sailors aboard the ship had bought the Cross, and that they had it with them. When the Cross was returned to Rreveli the ship's strange becalming ended and it was able to resume its passage.

Once rich, well endowed, and with considerable income from olives, cereals, fruit, honey, vegetables, cattle, sheep, goats and silkworms _ an extensive economic organisation _ the monastery survives today mainly on voluntary donations. In response to pleas for help, New Zealand ex-servicemen have been assisting in the preservation of a vanishing way of life. The monastery is magnificently sited with views over the libyan Sea. Below, the Megalopotamos River flows lazily south below a well preserved Venetian bridge. It was the retreat of some seventy-five monks half a century ago; today the monks' cells are empty and in residence are only two men - Abbot Kallinikos Spitadhakis II and Archimandritis Vasilios Dimitrakis. They blame the attractions of modern life and difficulties in attracting men into religious orders.

Yet Preveli attracts pilgrims from all over the world as tourists.

After the war there was the question of compensation for the people who had aided the New Zealanders who roamed the mountains. Soldiers could give Cretans chits for later redemption, but few kept these because if they were searched by Germans the chits became virtual death warrants.

Statements by servicemen helped to see that compensation went to the right people. But some Cretans who had done little or nothing were most active in pressing claims and several undeserving people received recognition. So disgusted were several of the most loyal patriots that they proudly declined to make claims.

Several servicemen who were stragglers feel that not enough was done to help people who had directly aided them.

Sympathetic post-war New Zealand governments, co-operating with servicemen's and relief organisations, gave limited assistance, providing food and clothing, and finance for childen's schooling. Successive governments drew the line at emigration unless prospective emigratnts had trade skills or werefound accommodation and work by sponsors. Consequently, many deserving Creatans were precluded - men who had risked life and limb and livelihood to help servicemen, some of whom survived with Cretan help for as long as two years. Other people who had had little or nothing to do with the stragglers were accepted as emigrants because they had a skill to offer and succeeded with sponsorship.

One man who tried to have the system changed was W. Martin, a lance-corporal, formerly of Waitakaruru, who spent all his personal savings in helping Cretans who had helped him and in trying to get more done for deserving Cretan families.

Left behind at Sphakia after the last evacuation ship had left, Martin was captured and imprisoned. He escaped and was sheltered by patriotic Cretans for two months before recapture to spend the rest of the war as a prisoner in Germany.

After the war he took his discharge in Crete and spent a year visiting the families who had helped him and other men on the run. In 1947 he returned to New Zealand with detailed news for other stragglers of how families who had helped them had fared during the Occupation and afterwards.

Such was his dedication that he went back to Crete in 1950, sought out hundreds of families and wrote thousands of letters to former stragglers and ex-prisoners in New Zealand, providing the latest information about their helpers. Many men remembered their helpers only by nicknames; Martin unravelled such puzzles and sent back correct addresses.

In cottages and remote villages a treasured possession was often a tattered photograph or other memento left by a New Zealander. As a result of Martin's reports, servicemen's and relief organisations mounted a national appeal for funds to help Cretans who found themselves in peacetime in distressed circumstances.

Martin formed a committee in Chanea of five trusted men whom he knew would distribute the aid fairly to the most deserving families. But he was thwarted by the Greek Consul in Wellington, who decided that the aid should be channelled through the Bishop of Chanea, a man regarded by Martin as rabidly anti-British and suspected of collaboration with the Germans during the Occupation.

Corruption was said to be rife at that time and little of the aid reached the people it was entended for. Màrtin said he spend 14 weeks trying to get the Bishop to release the supplies, without success. Then he had to leave and hitch-hike his way to London when his money ran out. Private parcels, however, were getting through to individual addresses and were gratefully received.

Ten years later, theproblem of immigration for Cretans remained; ex-servicement were still asking the Goverment to relax the rules to allow youths and girls from deserving families to enter the country.

A Hawke's Bay man, A.A. Madden, in 1961 found a way of bringing out Nicos Kindyannaki, the fifteen-year-old son of a Crrete family who helped him. He adopted the boy who was sponsored by the Waipukurau Rotary Club. After the lad's arrival Madden set about finding a way to bring out his family.

Not until forty years after the Battle of Crete were immigration laws relaxed to allow in "Greek families who have close ties with New Zealand service people as a result of thei wartime experiences". The Government offered to accept up to fifty families who had 'suffered considerable hardship because they assisted New Zealanders'. The Government acknowledged that some families had had their assets confiscated and children were brought up in poor circumstances.

For manny, this 'gesture of appreciation' came too late, their lives had already been lived, the prospect of a new life with prosperity lost. in the event only five families numbering twenty people availed themselves of the opportunity.

Meantime, over the years, ex-servicemen's organisations didnot forget. Money was collected constantly and sent to Crete to help the most deserving families, mostly for the education of their children. This assistance continues today.

Several other Cretans were luckier in getting acceptance and now some 350 from the island live in New Zealand. Some were sponsored by families who settled earlier, and not all stay for the rest of their lives. Most if not all have made a good livelihood in New Zealand and made valuable cultural contributions to the community. Some, reaching retirement, have elected to go back to the land of their birth, satisfied that life has treated them well, providing sufficient capital to live very comfortably in an island where conditions can still be hard and frugal in areas beyond the towns and tourist resorts.

One man who married a Cretan girl he met during his time as a straggler was Ian Begg. Captured by the Germans, he escaped and joined others in the hills. While hiding near the village of Neo Chorio, about twenty kilometres south-east of Chanea, he contracted hepatitis. Local people cared for him in an upstairs room of a house. One of the many who came to see him was a fourteen-year-old girl, Marika Lagonikakis. Feeling that large groups created confusion, Marika contrived to see Ian on his own, and strong feelings developed between them.

When he was fit again, Ian moved east disguised as a Greek. After tramping some fifty kilometres to Rethymnon he was questioned by German soldiers who discovered his identity through a book in English and letters in his possession. He spent the rest of the war as a prisoner in Germany and Poland, endured great hardships, survived a 'death march' in the final stages andwas repatriated weighing only thirty-eight kilograms. Back in New Zealand, Ian wrote to Marika in Crete, not knowing whether she had survived the German reprisal raids and executions. Seven months went by before he had her reply, the mails taking about fifteen weeks each way. Sh had not forgotten him. He telegraphed her to come to New Zealand and marry him. Her parents were more independent-minded and trusting than many Cretan families would have been, and she sailed off with their blessings.

To day, Ian and Marika live in A christchurch suburban home. A grapevine draped over a trellis outside the front door is a reminded of Cretan life. A battered German helmet is used to gather eggs from Marika's hens in the back garden, and a luxuriant olive tree is every year heavily laden.

Another New Zealander helped by Marika was Clive Hulme, then a sergeant, who earned the Victoria Cross for actions in Crete. Wounde, thirsty in intense heat, he staggered into Neo Chorio's village square. he asked two Greek soldiers at the well for water, but they showed him it was dry. marika at that moment came from a doorway into the square, and so he asked her. She

214

brought him a bowlful which he gratefully drank. Then she led him out of the village and pointed a route into the hills which would avoid advancing German troops. He reached Sphakia in time to be evacuated.

In 1975 Clive Hulme tried to find Marika in Crete where he learned of her emigration to New Zealand.

Marika's mother was also active in helping stragglers. With other women she helped to care for an Australian Norman Douglas Scott who was paralysed from the waist down. They kept him hidden in a small cave near Neo Chorio for two and half years before the Germans learned about him and took him prisoner. For her part in aiding the man, Marika's mother was awarded the George Medal.

Another who married into the family who assisted him while on the run was Corporal E.N.D. (Ned) Nathan of 28 Battalion. In the counter-attack on Maleme aerodrome he was wounded in the hip and eye. He was put on a barge carrying casualties to Egypt but it was sunk by enemy aircraft off Kastelli. Ned swam ashore, evaded German patrols and tried to make his way to the evacuation beach at Sphakia. He reached the south coast but found he was several kilometres west of his destination.

With his wounds troubling him. Nathan moved further west in Selino and met the Torakis family of Sklavopoula. Here he was nursed back to health. He learned the Cretan dialect and for many months moved freely about. German soldiers took him to be a Cretan and twice, when questioned by the Gestapo he convinced them too that he was Greek. Questioned a third time by the Gestapo, after being captured by an Austrian patrol near Promodi on 23 May 1942, he was not so lucky; his identity was established and he was badly beaten up when he refused to reveal who had benn harbouring him. By this time he was engaged to a daughter of the family, Katina.

In Chania general hospital for treatment. After his capture, he was visited by Fifi. Sh was given special permission to see him and another new Zealander, Joe Angel.

Later, from prison cmp in Germany, Nathan wrote to Katina in Sklavopoula. The Gestapo heard about the letter and Hans Wachter interrogated the Torakis family about Katina's relationship with Ned. Wachter was told that Katina had met Ned in Chania before the Nazi invasion and Wachter reluctantly accepted this stpry. Because of his bad eye Ned was repatriated eight months before the war ended. He went back to Crete and married to girl to whom he was betrothed. The couple lived in Dargaville, North Auckland, where Ned died on August 17 August, 1987, aged 67. Earlier in the year he had been awarded the C.B.E. (Commander of the British Empire) for his service to many public, Maori and charitable causes. For eleven years he was national president of the 28th Maori Battalion.

And now what will become of us without barbarians?
These people were a kind of solution.

- Cretan *rizitika*

Half a century after the epic World War Two Battle of Crete the people treat the anniversary commemorations, still held, with great ceremony, more as a festival. "Celebration" is the word used on posters, plastered prominently in public places as 20 May draws near.

What the islanders did, aided by New Zealand, British and Australian troops, both during and after the battle, is regarded with pride. Cretans honour their dead, centrainly. Services are held, wreaths are laid on memorials and at cemeteries. But, after that, what is celebrated is the close kinship established during the fighting and the occupation. New Zealand, Australian and British visitors on these occasion, many of them veterans of the battle, contantly enjoy an experience they say will never forget the open-hearted hospitality of a Cretan community which seems determined never to forget the men of the Commonwealth who came so far to help them against a determined and ruthless enemy.

These days many Cretans are prepared to forgive their oppressors, even if they cannot forget. Since the island opened to tourism Germans have been coming in ever-increasing numbers and their presence has contributed to Crete's prosperity.

Occasionally old foes meet as friends. A British sergeant, visiting the German cemetery, was greeted by a former German soldier. "I remember you", he said. "You saved my life. Your men were going to shoot me, but you ordered them not to. "I'm very grateful.

BIBLIOGRAPHY

Auckland Weekly News, Articles 2 May 1951; July 1951.

Charman, Paul. Submarine Torbay.

Robert Hale, London, 1989.

Clark, Alan. *The Fall of Crete*, Anthony Blond Ltd, 1962.

Comeau, G.M. *Operation Mercury*. Kimber, 1961.

Courtney, G.B. *SBS in World War Two*. Robert Hale Ltd, London, 1983.

Davin, D.M. *Official New Zealand War History* - Crete 1953.

Dawkins, R.M. *Folk Memory in Crete*. Folklore, 1930.
Soul and Body in Greek Folklore. Folklore, 1942.

Doren, David MacNeil. the Winds of Crete. John Murray, 1974.

Details supplied by New Zealand Ministry of Defence, Wellington, New Zealand.

Fielding, Xan. Hide and Seek. martin Secker and Warburg, 1955.
The Stronghold. Secker and Warburg, 1953.

Hadjipateras, Costas N. and Fafalios, Marias. Crete 1941 Eyewitnessed. Efstathiadis Group, Athens, 1989.

Foot, M.R.D. and Langley, J.M. Miq escape and evasion 1939-1945. Bodley Head 1979.

Hammond, Nicholas. *Venture Into Greece*. William Kimber and Co., London, 1983.

Harokopos, G. *The Fortress Crete 1941-1944*. George Evangelios, Athens, 1971.

Hopkins, Adam. *Grete - Its Past, Present and People*. Faber and Faber, 1977.

Johnson, B. *The Secret War*. BBC Publications, London, 1978.

Jordan, William. *Conquest Without Victory*. Hodder and Stoughton, 1969.

Kiriakopoulos, G.C. Ten days to destiny. Franklin Watts, New York, 1985.

Lewin, R. *Ultra Goes to War*. hutchinson, London, 1978.

Manuscript by David and Judy Mitchell. 'Homage to Crete'.

Manuscript by D. G. Buchanan, Dunedin, New Zealand.

Mason, W. Wynne. *Prisoners of War*. Goverment Printer, Wellington, 1954.

Moss, W. Stanley. *Ill Met by Moonlight*. George G. Harrap and Co. Ltd, 1950.

Natopoulos, J.A. 'Homer and Cretan Heroic Poetry'. American *Journal of Philosophy* Vol. LXXIII, 1952.

New Zealand Crete Veterans Association magazines and newsletters.

Pitt, Barrie. Special boat squadron. Century publishing, London 1983.

Psychoundakis, George. *The Cretan Runner* (trans. Patrick Leigh Fermor). John Murray, 1955.

Ragovin, F. *Cretan Mantinades* (song poems). S. Halkiandakis, 1974.

Rendel, A.M. *Appointment in Crete*. Allan Wingate, 1953.

Royal Air Force War Office and Special Operations Executive files at the Public Record Office, Kew, London.

Sey Mour, William. British special forces. Sidswiek and Jackson, 1985.

Simpson, Tony. *Operation Mercury*. hodder and Stoughton, 1981.

Smith, Michael Llewellyn. *The Great Island*. Allen Lane, 1965.

Stephanides, Theodore. *Climax in Crete*. Faber and Faber, 1946.

Stewart, I. McD. G. *The Struggle for Crete*. Oxford University Press, 1966.

Von der Heydte, Baron. Daedalus Returned. Hutchinson, 1958.

Winterbotham, F.W. *The Ultra Secret*. Weidenfeld and Nicholson, London 1974.

Woodhouse, C.M. *Apple of Discord*. Hutchinson, 1948.

Interviews (taped and translated) with:
Vasili Paterakis, in Souyia, Grete
Manoli Paterakis, in Koustoyérako Crete
Andonis Paterakis, in Koystoyérako and Souyia, Crete
Vardis Paterakis in Koystoyérako and Souyia, Crete
Costis Paterakis, in Koystoyérako and Chanea, Crete
Yanni Zambiakos, in Koystoyérako and Chanea, Crete
Pavlo Vernadakis, in Chanea, Crete
Georgiow Kandanoleon, in Koystoyérako Crete
Panayiotis Tsamandakis, in Wellington, New Zealand.

Meeting and talks with:
Major Xan Fielding, DSO, S.O.E., author of *Hide and Seek* and The
Stronghold, in London
Major Sandy (A.M.) Rendel S.O.E., at Alderbury Wiltshire
George Psychoundakis, author of *The Cretan Runner*, in Maleme,
Crete
Antonis Kosmadakis, President, Crete-New Zealand Association in
Chanea, Crete
Major Dennis Ciclitira, S.O.E., in London.

Interviews, corrspondence or consultation with:
Major Jack Smith-Hughes, OBE, S.O.E., living in the British
Virgin islands
Captain John Stanley, I.S.L.D., Waldingham, Surrey
Major Ralph Stockbridge, OBE, MC, I.S.L.D., Royston,
Hertfordshire.

In New Zealand:

J.W. Bain Ern	W. Rogers
Jim McDevitt	W.H. Gill

Richard (Bert) Dyson
Geoff Gunn
Vic Rowland
Ian Johnston
Philip McConnell
Ralph A. Holmes
Dorothy Perkins
Nevilli Perkins
Jack Perkins
Dudley Moir

Robert A. Holmes
Arthur Helm
Marika Begg
Ned Nathan
Fifi (Papantonakis) Griggs
Ron Jenner
Joan Kerr
B.L. McDonald
R.W. Rolfe

Documentary letters written by:
John Kerr 14/8/51
R.W. Rolfe 15/12/51

W.M. Rowland 20/4/42
Jim McDevitt 25/5/47